Worship Inside And Out

A Biblical Theology For Worship

Joel Williams

Worship Inside And Out: A Biblical Theology For Worship
ISBN: Softcover 978-1-955581-25-7
Copyright © 2021 by Joel Williams

All rights reserved. No part of this book may be reproduced or transmitted in any form or by any means, electronic or mechanical, including photocopying, recording, or by any information storage and retrieval system, without permission in writing from the publisher.

Scripture quotations are from the ESV® Bible (The Holy Bible, English Standard Version®), copyright © 2001 by Crossway, a publishing ministry of Good News Publishers. Used by permission. All rights reserved.

Parson's Porch Books is an imprint of Parson's Porch *&* Company (PP*&*C) in Cleveland, Tennessee. PP*&*C is an innovative organization which raises money by publishing books of noted authors, representing all genres. Its face and voice is **David Russell Tullock** (dtullock@parsonsporch.com).

Parson's Porch *&* Company *turns books into bread & milk* by sharing its profits with the poor.

www.parsonsporch.com

Worship Inside And Out

Contents

Introduction 7
Chapter 1: 11
   What is Worship?
Chapter 2: 30
   Offering and Sacrifice
Chapter 3: 45
   Prayer
Chapter 4: 63
   Praise
Chapter 5: 82
   The Word
Chapter 6: 98
   The Lord's Supper
Conclusion 111
Worshipers 112
Worship Leaders 118
Bibliography 121
About the Author 123

Introduction

"I can see clearly now!" For generations before the year 2020, most of us only associated the term "2020" with vision. Generally speaking, those with 20/20 vision are considered to have normal eyesight. They can see objects clearly at a distance of 20 feet, which must be a wonderful feeling! For years, I've fallen into the camp of those who don't have normal vision. For me to be able to see clearly at 20 feet -- or less than two feet -- I need glasses to correct my vision. Glasses filter the world around me to help my eyes and brain work together to process things more clearly. Without my glasses, things look blurry. Details are missing. My understanding of who or what I see is unsure. I can easily get confused or even deceived by what I think I see when I don't have on my glasses. But once I put on my glasses, my vision is corrected. I can see clearly. Things aren't blurry. Details are present. My understanding of who or what I see is sure. I don't easily get confused or even deceived by what I see when I have on my glasses.

For me -- and perhaps most of us -- the year 2020 was a year of putting on new glasses and seeing some things more clearly. We didn't plan it that way. It just happened. The pandemic hit us like a blindside tackle. Within weeks, our world changed. Most of us found ourselves working from home for a while. Many found themselves unable to work, as businesses closed their doors and lay-offs rapidly escalated. Schools were shuttered, leaving teachers scrambling to move their classrooms online, and the basic supplies we needed for cleaning and protection couldn't be found in the stores that were still open in our communities. For the first time in our lives, churches in our states were told to close their doors. Hopefully for the last time in our lives, churches in most communities weren't able to come together in person to worship on Easter Sunday! Everything in our lives seemed blurry. All the details weren't present. We were confused and wondering if we might even be deceived. Everything had changed.

The pandemic would be enough, but as the old saying goes, bad things usually happen in threes. I don't know if that's true, but it at least seemed to be doubly true in 2020. With an already contentious presidential election underway, social unrest spread across the United States in the wake of the death of George Floyd, leading us into a summer that was hot politically and socially. For those of us on the gulf coast, natural disaster after natural disaster was added to the mix, as one of the busiest hurricane seasons in decades hit our country. There were fires and earthquakes in the west, and there was snow all over! For all of us, the year 2020 was a tough year. It was a year that stretched and strained us in various ways, but it was a year that also allowed some of us to see some things come into focus. From family time to finances and from social issues to the church, we all had to do some straining to get focus.

The situation of 2020 was the impetus of this book. This book is the result of some straining that we did in our church to get focus on one important issue: Worship. The chapters that follow come out of the response to a simple question that we asked as our church faced the pandemic restrictions: "How can we continue to be faithful in being the church during a time when we are restricted in physically gathering to worship as the church?"

The question isn't new, and it's not unique. In many areas around the world where gathering as the church is restricted for political and/or religious reasons, this question has already been asked. The church has already wrestled with the answer. God's Word has already planted its truth in the heart of the church. For the church in the United States, however, where we've enjoyed so much freedom and protection in our ability to gather and to worship, the question maybe didn't need to be asked in the past. That's not necessarily a good thing. For me, not asking the question clearly enough led to some blurriness in my understanding and approach to worship. When we don't have to think about why we do what we do, we tend to just keep doing what we've always done. It's not until we can't do what we've always done as the church that we're really challenged to start looking at the why of what we've been doing.

Why do we do the things that we do in worship? When it comes to the issue of worship, the year 2020 made me step back and really ask this question. It forced me to begin to deeply explore how God's Word answers that question. During the period of time that our church couldn't physically gather, we wanted our church to continue to be faithful. During the period of time that we were gathering together under cleaning, masking, and social distancing restrictions, we wanted our church to be faithful. How do we do that? What does it really mean to worship, and what are the essential expressions of biblical worship? How does God define worship, and how have God's people displayed faithfulness in worshiping God throughout the biblical period of history until today?

As I began to wrestle with these issues, our song leader asked me a simple question: "Can you do a sermon series on worship?" We were making changes in our worship service times and format to accommodate worship and small groups on Sunday mornings during the pandemic, and the changes were requiring some sacrifice and adjustment from our church. We had planned a worship series in the past, but for some reason, we had never done it. This was the time. Our church needed a reminder of what worship is and how we're called to faithfully express our worship to the Lord. This book is the result of months of study and prayer that led to that sermon series on worship in 2020. This was a time of putting on new glasses for me, and it was a time of seeing worship more clearly through the lens of God's Word.

So if you have all the answers about what worship is and how we should express our worship to God, this book is not for you. However, if things are still a little blurry, and worship is still an issue in your church -- or perhaps even in your heart -- then this book is for you. My prayer is that God's Word will help bring biblical worship into focus in your head and in your heart. My hope is that this will be a book that reinforces truths that you know; reminds you of truths that you may have forgotten; and reveals to you truths that you need to embrace. Worship should be what brings God's people together and brings great glory to our God. Father, teach us to worship!

Chapter 1:
What is Worship?

When I was a child and into my early teens, I played baseball and basketball, and I even boxed. There were two things that were true about my attempts to play these sports. First, I wasn't very good. I enjoyed playing the games. I even imagined myself making great plays, but the reality of what I wanted to do and what I could do just didn't match-up. Second, I didn't read a single sentence from the rule book for any of these sports. I simply learned how to play the game by watching others play the game. All that I understood about baseball and basketball came from my experience of watching the game being played, playing the game myself, and having people tell me that "this is the way it's played." In and of itself, this isn't a bad thing. This is how we learn about and learn how to do much of what we know and do in life. However, it's also not the best thing. There are dangers to this method of learning.

One danger is that we learn some of what we need to know, but we don't learn all that we need to know to play the game well or even properly. There's a lot I really didn't know when it came to playing each of those sports. I made mistakes that I would not have made if I had really known and understood the rules of the game, and I often learned things the hard way by doing things the wrong way. Another danger -- which is perhaps the greatest danger -- is learning the wrong rules and techniques for the game. Learning the game from watching others play the game is only as good as the ability of those playing the game to play it correctly, and it's also dependent on my ability to correctly understand what they are doing.

My guess is that many of us learn about worship in the same way. We learn from watching and participating much more than from studying God's Word to develop a biblical understanding of worship. While learning by watching and participating isn't necessarily bad -- in fact, it's necessary -- learning only by watching and participating does come with some possible pitfalls. This method only works if the worship we watch is true, biblical worship, and even if that's the case, the method only works when we are able to rightly interpret the worship we watch. But even in the case of watching and rightly interpreting good, biblical worship, there's another pitfall in only learning the how and not the why of worship. By watching and participating, we're prone to learn how to worship in a particular way, but we're also prone not to understand why we worship in that particular way. This is what I believe leads to the "because we've always done it this way" mentality when it comes to worship. In the heart of someone who knows the how of worship but not the why of worship, the style of music, the elements of the service, and the aesthetics and organization of the gathering space for worship often become more about preference and familiarity than about theological conviction.

My prayer is that this book will help lay a biblical foundation to reinforce and to develop theological convictions about why we do what we do in worship, but before we explore the ways we express worship, we need to begin at a more basic level by defining worship. What is worship? To define what worship is we'll explore two things. First, we'll look at the biblical words that are used for worship, and second, we'll look at a few passages that utilize those words for worship as well as some passages that give us pictures or examples of proper expressions of worship. Hopefully, putting the basic meaning of "worship" words together with examples of acceptable worship will give us a biblical picture of the heart of worship through the hearts of worshippers as God recorded them for us in his Word.

The Language of Worship

In my undergraduate work in college, one of my professors told me that some classes are just "jumping through hoops." In other words, it didn't matter if you liked the class or not, you just had to jump through the hoop of completing the class to get to the other side. For some of you, this short section on biblical words may be a hoop to jump through, but for others, it may be a steak to feast on. As we briefly look at some Hebrew and Greek words related to worship, the purpose is not to teach us Hebrew or Greek; rather, the purpose is to help us grow in our understanding of what biblical worship really is. So jump through the hoop! But I also hope that you'll savor the meat that's there.

In the language of the Old Testament, we'll look at four, Hebrew words that are used in connection to worship. First, the worship word most commonly used (289 times) in the Old Testament is the word עָבַד (transliterated "abad" in English). The most common definition of this word is "to work" or "to serve." It's often used in connection with the work and service done for the Lord, but the use of this word in Scripture is not limited to working and to serving the Lord God alone. It's also used in connection with worship of false gods. In Deuteronomy 7:16, God's people are commanded and warned not to "serve" the gods of the people that they will soon conquer in the Promised Land. The word is additionally used in connection to service and to work that is performed for kings and rulers. It refers to the service given by or forced on subjects of a king and slaves of a master. The word is connected to action. It's about work and service that is performed.[1]

Second, the word שָׁחָה (transliterated "shachah" in English) is used 172 times in the Old Testament. The basic meaning of the word is "to bow down" or literally "to prostrate" oneself on the ground. In connection with the worship of God, this word captures a physical posture that is intended to reveal an inward posture of humility, submission, gratefulness, or -- in a word -- worship. In Genesis 24:26, when the servant of Abraham was led to Abraham's family in search of a wife for the son of Abraham, Isaac, the servant bowed his head and worshipped! In a moment, the man's physical, outward posture and his spiritual, inward posture indicated grateful humility before the Lord. The word is also used to indicate the appropriate and rightful posture of all people before the Lord. Isaiah pointed to the time when the haughty and proud would be bowed down before the Lord.[2] This beautifully rich, Old Testament word provides a powerfully visual illustration of what worship should be inwardly in the hearts of men and women.[3]

Third, the word שָׁרַת (transliterated "sharath" in English) essentially means "to minister" or "to serve." This word is used 97 times in the Old Testament, and it's used both in connection to servants of the Lord as well as to those who serve idols and other people. In Genesis 39:4, Joseph served Potiphar in Egypt. In 1 Kings 8:11, the Levites weren't able to enter into the temple to serve or to minister because the glory of the Lord filled the new temple in Jerusalem. This word is often used in connection to the service of priests in the

---

[1] See Deut. 7:16 (ESV) and https://biblehub.com/hebrew/5647.htm.
[2] Isa. 2:11 and 17.
[3] See Gen. 24:26 and https://biblehub.com/hebrew/7812.htm.

administration of their priestly duties.⁴ The final and fourth word is only used in Isaiah 44 and 46 in connection with idol worship. The word is סָגַד (transliterated "sagad" in English) and similar to shachah, this word means "to fall prostrate" on the ground in worship.⁵

As we move into the New Testament, there are five words for worship that continue to reinforce the basic definitions that we find in the Old Testament. First, the most common word for worship, used 60 times in the New Testament, is προσκυνέω (transliterated proskuneo). Similar to shachah, the word carries the idea of falling down or prostrating oneself on the ground. It literally means "to kiss towards" someone, showing adoration and respect to a superior. This word brings a powerful picture of submission, adoration, and respect into the act of worship, and it ties the physical posture of the worshipper to the expression of their inward posture before God. This is the term for worship that Jesus used in John 4 when he spoke to the Samaritan woman at the well about the true worship of God that will be in spirit and in truth.⁶

Second, the word λατρεύω (transliterated latreuo in English) is used 21 times in the New Testament. Like "abad" in the Hebrew, this Greek word fundamentally means "to serve" or "to work." It's used to point to the service or work of a servant or slave for his or her master and in relation to the worship of God, Luke commonly used this word in his New Testament books to describe believers who served and worshiped the Lord with their lives.⁷ Latreuo evokes the

---

[4] See Gen. 39:4 and https://biblehub.com/hebrew/8334.htm.
[5] See Isa. 44:12-17 and https://biblehub.com/hebrew/5456.htm.
[6] See John 4:21-24 and https://biblehub.com/greek/4352.htm.
[7] Luke 1:74, 2:37, 4:8; Acts 7:7, 24:14, 27:23.

image of action in the lives of those who serve and work for the Lord.[8]

Third, the word σέβομαι (transliterated in the root "sebo") is another word for worship that is used 10 times in the New Testament. This word simply means "to worship" or "to have reverence," and in the New Testament, it often is used in connection to Gentiles who fear the Lord, the God of Israel.[9] Fourth, the word λειτουργέω (transliterated "leitourgeo") is used three times in the New Testament to describe the ministry of God's servants. Much like sharath, this word is connected to the work of ministry. It's the word that we get our modern day word "liturgy" from, which describes the very elements and order of public worship today,[10] and finally, the fifth word is θρησκεία (transliterated "threskeia" in English), which is used four times in the New Testament and connected to a primary meaning of religion or piousness. James used this word to define pure and undefiled "religion."[11]

While a study of words alone will only provide us with a small glimpse into the biblical meaning of worship, these words do give us an important glimpse. What we see consistently in these words, which capture worship in various ways and in two very different languages, is that worship is active and not passive. Worship naturally moves from the inside to the outside of a person's life. In other words, worship isn't just a belief, a feeling, or a thought; rather, worship is a belief, a feeling, or a thought that is expressed in action. Worship is expressed in service, singing, ministry, prayer, praise,

---

[8] See Luke 1:67-79 and https://biblehub.com/greek/3000.htm.
[9] See Acts 16:14 and https://biblehub.com/greek/4576.htm.
[10] See Acts 13:2 and https://biblehub.com/greek/3008.htm.
[11] See Jas. 1:27 and https://biblehub.com/greek/2356.htm.

surrender, thanksgiving and much more, but worship is not just the action either. Action for God with your hands is not worship if the action of your heart towards God isn't worship. True worship is both on the inside and outside of our lives. Worship is our outward posture towards God that flows from our inward posture before God.

Examples of Worship

Words alone aren't enough to give us the full definition of worship. In fact, as we've already seen, we need examples of a word being used in context in order to get an idea of the range of meaning for that word. Thankfully, the Lord provided hundreds of examples of worship words used in connection with examples of worship in the lives of his people. In this section, we'll explore some worship words used in Scripture as well as some examples of worship found in God's Word. Hopefully, God will help us continue to piece together a clear understanding of what worship is.

Starting in Genesis, worship words are consistently connected to the revelation of God and the subsequent response of God's people to that revelation. Specifically, the response of God's people is seen -- early and often -- in bowing before the Lord in worship. This symbol of bowing or putting one's face to the ground was the symbol of submission before a figure of authority, such as a king. It was an indication of submission, honor, and recognition to the ruler. Bowing is an incredibly vulnerable position that literally puts one's life at the feet of another. For the people of God, as they recognized God's revelation of himself, which came through things such as answered prayer and which was even dramatically seen in manifestations of the Lord's presence with them, the common response was one of reverential fear and honor, bowing before the

Lord with thanksgiving for answered prayers and with hearts of honor and acknowledgement before the Creator God.

We are presented with this very response the first time that a worship word is connected to an example of worship in Genesis. In the case of Abraham's servant, who went to look for a wife for Abraham's son, Isaac, we see that when the Lord brought him straight to the family of Abraham, answering his prayer for success for his master, "the man bowed his head and worshiped the LORD."[12] Later in the passage, the story was recounted as the man told Abraham's kinsman the following:

> Then I bowed my head and worshiped the LORD and blessed the LORD, the God of my master Abraham, who had led me by the right way to take the daughter of my master's kinsman for his son.[13]

We see this pattern continued not only in the lives of individuals who worshiped God, but also in the lives of the people of God as they corporately and collectively responded to the revelation of God. In the book of Exodus, when Moses returned to Egypt with the message that the Lord had visited his people and had seen their affliction, the people of Israel responded in the following manner: "They bowed their heads and worshiped."[14] When God gave Israel the Passover as an observance of his deliverance, once again the people of Israel "bowed their heads and worshiped."[15]

---

[12] Gen. 24:26.
[13] Gen. 24:48.
[14] Exod. 4:31.
[15] Exod. 12:27.

This same internal to external expression of worship is also seen in worship that wasn't directed to the Lord, as people are often seen bowing down and worshiping idols, such as in Isaiah 44. In fact, even Jesus, when he was on the earth, was tempted by Satan to bow down and to worship Satan in exchange for a false promise of power and authority on earth.[16] Consistently, the use of the word "worship" in Scripture is used in connection to bowing in humble submission and grateful recognition of the Lord, which is reinforced in the final book of the Bible in some of the most dramatic scenes of worship. In these scenes of worship in heaven, the twenty-four elders, the angels, and the four living creatures fall down on their faces and worship God!

> . . . the twenty-four elders fall down before him who is seated on the throne and worship him who lives forever and ever. They cast their crowns before the throne . . .[17]
>
> And the four living creatures said, 'Amen!' and the elders fell down and worshiped.[18]
>
> And all the angels were standing around the throne and around the elders and the four living creatures, and they fell on their faces before the throne and worshiped God . . .[19]

---

[16] Matt. 4:9.
[17] Rev. 4:10.
[18] Rev. 5:14.
[19] Rev. 7:11.

> And the twenty-four elders who sit on their thrones before God fell on their faces and worshiped God . . .[20]

When all of these examples are put together, we see clearly that worship must involve a humble submission to the one, true God. It seems to always flow from a grateful recognition of who the Lord is and what the Lord has done. Worship is expressed outwardly, but it's the inward condition of the heart towards the Lord that makes the outward expression to the Lord true worship. Perhaps this is most vividly seen in the life of our Lord Jesus when he was praying in the garden before his arrest and crucifixion. In Luke 22, Jesus is the example of submission and recognition before the Lord. He fell down on the ground and prayed, "not my will, but your will be done."[21]

When was the last time you fell on your face before the Lord? For many of us, this is foreign to our experience in life. In our culture in the United States, we're taught to stand up straight. We're supposed to look people in the eyes and shake their hand with strength and confidence. We don't bow down to others. We aren't supposed to look away in deference to others, but certainly, this doesn't apply to our Lord! Throughout the history of Christian worship, elements of these physical expressions of worship have always been present: Bowing our heads, kneeling down, and even falling face down on the ground before the Lord.

Now, there's nothing magical about the acts of bowing or kneeling down. There's nothing supernatural about the act of laying prostrate

---

[20] Rev. 11:16.
[21] Luke 22:39-46.

on the ground; however, when these physical expressions of worship truly express the condition of our hearts before the Lord, they can be powerful reminders to us of our proper posture before the Lord. Remember, before the church of Jesus was instituted and before the nation of Israel was established, there were individuals who recognized God. They knew he existed. They experienced his presence and his power. They were recipients of his provision and grace, and in response to the revelation of the Lord, they bowed down and worshiped.

Without humble submission and grateful recognition of the Lord, any action or expression of worship fails to be true worship before the one, true King. Worship starts and ends in the heart. Worship is a submitted heart that recognizes that the Lord is God and that gives the Lord God the obedience, recognition, and honor that he deserves.

So, if worship requires humble submission and grateful recognition of the Lord, what does this look like in your personal worship? What does it look like in corporate worship in your church? Take a minute to bow down, kneel down, or lay prostrate, and ask the Lord to give you discernment into how the outward expressions of your worship point to the inward reality of worship in your heart. Then come back to this page to work through the following questions:

>(1) What are the physical expressions of worship that you use in your personal or private worship?

>(2) What do these expressions of worship reveal about your heart's position or posture before the Lord? Do they accurately represent your inward expression of worship to the Lord?

> (3) What are the physical expressions of worship that your church uses in corporate worship?
>
> (4) What are some of the inward conditions of the heart that these outward expressions of worship are intended to display? Are there outward expressions of worship that are missing or perhaps would be considered inappropriate in your corporate worship? Why?

Worship is not only seen in Scripture where worship words are connected to the worship actions of people, but worship is also seen in specific acts of worship in the lives of God's people. In fact, the earliest pictures of expressions of worship in Scripture remind us that worship is -- most basically -- a response to the revelation of God and what he has done. One of the first stories of worship is a story about the offering and sacrifice given to God by Cain and Abel. In Genesis 4, we're told that Cain and Abel were the sons of the first man and the first woman: Adam and Eve. Abel was a keeper of sheep, and Cain was a farmer. As the Lord provided harvest from their flock and field, here's what happened:

> In the course of time Cain brought to the LORD an offering of the fruit of the ground, and Abel also brought of the firstborn of his flock and of their fat portions. And the LORD had regard for Abel and his offering, but for Cain and his offering he had no regard . . . .[22]

While there's much to be learned about acceptable and unacceptable acts of worship in this story, both Cain and Abel were responding to

---

[22] Gen. 4:3-5a.

God's provision. They were worshiping by offering and sacrificing to the Lord as a response to what he had done in giving new life in Abel's flock and in providing produce in Cain's field.

A few chapters later, in Genesis 8, the Lord provides a portrait of worship in the lives of Noah and his family after they were delivered through the flood. Once the waters receded and Noah and his family were able to leave the ark onto dry ground, the first thing that they did was build an altar and offer sacrifices to the Lord.

> Then Noah built an altar to the LORD and took some of every clean animal and some of every clean bird and offered burnt offerings on the altar. And when the LORD smelled the pleasing aroma, the LORD said in his heart, "I will never again curse the ground because of man, for the intention of man's heart is evil from his youth. Neither will I ever again strike down every living creature as I have done."[23]

Quickly following the story of Noah, the pattern of revelation and response continued in the life of Abraham. When God visited Abraham and revealed his covenant and blessing through Abraham, Abraham responded by building an altar and offering sacrifices to the Lord.

> Abram passed through the land to the place of Shechem, to the oak of Moreh. At that time the Canaanites were in the land. Then the LORD appeared to Abram and said, "To your offspring I

---

[23] Gen. 8:20-21.

> will give this land." So he built there an altar to the
> LORD, who had appeared to him.[24]

Yet another example is when Moses led God's people out of Egypt. After the Lord parted the sea for Israel to cross over on dry ground, the Lord then completely destroyed Pharoah and his army in the sea, as the parted waters closed together around them and drowned them. Moses responded by leading God's people in a song of praise to God for his deliverance from Egypt.

> Thus the LORD saved Israel that day from the hand of the Egyptians, and Israel saw the Egyptians dead on the seashore. Israel saw the great power that the LORD used against the Egyptians, so the people feared the LORD, and they believed in the LORD and in his servant Moses. Then Moses and the people of Israel sang this song to the Lord . . .[25]

While we could go on-and-on, the point is that Scripture reveals a clear pattern in true worship: As God reveals himself to his people, the appropriate response to his revelation is worship!

This brings up a really important point. In all of these pictures of early worship in Scripture, God recounted individuals as well as groups of people who worshiped him in a variety of ways, but the thing that connected all of these expressions of worship is that they were all timely responses from the hearts of God's people to give the Lord thanks and praise for who he was and for what he had done. Here's the main point that we must remember: Worship is God-

---

[24] Gen. 12:6-7.
[25] Exod. 14:30-15:1.

focused, and worship is meant to be a regular rhythm in our lives, actively responding to who God is and what God is doing.

In considering all of this, there are at least a couple of reasons why some believers have trouble in worship. Perhaps the most significant reason is that their worship isn't truly a rhythm in their lives. Throughout the week, in the regular rhythms of life, they've failed to see how God has given them life, work, food, clothes, family, friends, education, comfort, entertainment, mercy, joy, etc. They haven't lived their week responding to God's revelation by worshiping him. They have lived their lives disconnected from worship, which has been segmented to this one area of life that generally happens on Sunday mornings. They come to a church service after a worshipless week expecting worship to be served up like the pot roast they'll eat for lunch after the service. If the music is good and the preacher does his job, their souls will be filled up and satisfied. The expectation is that God will "show up and fill me up."

If this in fact happens in the life of a believer, then the second issue may be a problem as well: Their worship isn't focused on God! If they can't worship because the instruments or the songs aren't the instruments or songs that they like, then their worship may be more self-focused than God-focused. If they couldn't worship because the lights were turned off (or on!) or because the preacher went a few minutes too long, then perhaps they are coming to get something from worship rather than to give something to God through worship.

However, when we truly focus on God in worship it leads to true worship. Personal worship can happen wherever we are and in whatever we're doing. As we see God's presence at work in our lives and in the lives of others, we can bow our heads and worship. When we are reminded of his answered prayers and his promises, we can bow our heads and worship. When we read or hear his Word and know he's speaking to us, we can bow our heads and worship. The same is true when we gather corporately. God is the true focus in worship. D.A. Carson stated it this way in his book *Worship by the Book*:

> What ought to make worship delightful to us is not, in the first instance, its novelty or its aesthetic beauty, but its object: God himself is delightfully wonderful, and we learn to delight in him.[26]

The Lord was very gracious in giving me a wife who is an excellent cook. I've never had to worry about cooking because Tiffany has always enjoyed taking care of our family in this way. However, her enjoyment may not have continued if my enjoyment of her food wasn't appropriately responsive. If I was constantly nitpicking her food, complaining if the peas had gotten a little cold or if the meat had a little too much salt for my taste, she might lose her joy in cooking for me. If I never complimented her food or never expressed that I was enjoying what she cooked, she might lose interest in cooking for me. If I was constantly rejecting her food and then complaining about how hungry I was, she might completely lose her patience with me. If I never said "thank you" for the meal that she took time to prepare, she would likely be deeply hurt by me.

Isn't this exactly what happens when worship becomes self-focused rather than God-focused? A symptom of self-focused worship is often a selfish pursuit and imbalanced focus on preferences in

---

[26] D. A. Carson, *Worship by the book* (Grand Rapids: Zondervan, 2002), 30.

expressions of worship. This doesn't mean, however, that our expressions of worship don't matter. They do! Our expressions of worship must be acceptable to God, but for worship to be worship, the pursuit and focus of worship must be God.

This leads us to another aspect of worship, which will be our final consideration in defining worship: Worship involves both your spirit and your mind. This is important. The worship wars aren't new. There have always been worship wars among those who claim to worship God, and a major worship war developed thousands of years ago when the kingdom of Israel divided into the northern kingdom (Israel) and the southern kingdom (Judah). Initially, the Jews in Judah had the truth. They had worship that was based on the law that God gave them through Moses. They had the sacrifices, festivals, and the temple in Jerusalem, which was the dwelling place of God among his people and the appointed place for gathering for worship and sacrifice. However, through the time of the divided kingdom and finally after the return from exile, the northern kingdom, Israel, instituted and maintained worship that was outside of the law, actually changing God's Word to justify their worship on Mt. Gerizim. They sacrificed outside of the temple in Jerusalem, claiming that it was now their true place of worship.

So at the time of Jesus, there was worship in Samaria that some claimed to be true worship, which surely included many people who had very genuine convictions about their worship. Yet, their worship was devoid of truth. On the other hand, there was worship in Judah under the divided kingdom and after the return from exile that was full of the truth, but it was devoid of a genuine spirit of worship. In Jerusalem, they ended up going through the motions, but the spirit of their worship was far from God, as was finally and glaringly displayed in the fact that they failed to see and to accept the very presence of God with them in Christ Jesus.

So when Jesus encountered a Samaritan woman at a well, his words were incredible and incredibly important:

> Jesus said to her, "Woman, believe me, the hour is coming when neither on this mountain nor in Jerusalem will you worship the Father. You worship what you do not know; we worship what we know, for salvation is from the Jews. But the hour is coming, and is now here, when the true worshipers will worship the Father in spirit and truth, for the Father is seeking such people to worship him. God is spirit, and those who worship him must worship in the spirit and truth."[27]

Spirit and truth are not mutually exclusive; they are necessarily connected. Worship is not just an emotion that you feel in your spirit. Our feelings can be fickle, and our emotions can be deceiving. Worship is much more than a feeling even though feeling is certainly part of worship. We can experience and feel something in what we may call worship, but if it is contradictory to God's truth, then it fails to be worship that is acceptable to God. So this leads to the element of truth.

The truth is important, but the truth is that truth alone can lead to arrogance and pride. As a result, worship is not just truth either. Worship is more than just truth, even though it is not less than truth. Truth is an absolute necessity for true worship; however, worship

---

[27] John 4:21-24.

requires both spirit and truth. True worship is from the heart, expressing humble submission and grateful recognition of God, and true worship must be in response to the truth, expressed in a way that is consistent with God's design and desire for our worship. Are these two things in balance in your worship? Take a minute to prayerfully answer the questions below as they relate to both your private and corporate worship.

Applying God's Truth

(1) What does it mean to worship in spirit?

(2) What does it mean to worship in truth?

(3) Why are both of these things essential for our worship to be acceptable to the Lord?

Chapter 2:
Offering and Sacrifice

When I completed my graduate work at Louisiana State University, President George Bush was the speaker at the graduation ceremony. I was not only a graduate student at the university, but I was also a fulltime employee of the university. Being on campus, I had the privilege of hearing a little bit about the preparation for President Bush's visit. It started weeks in advance when the President's advance team came onto campus to begin working through all of the security planning and assessing all of the security risks. They identified potential threats, and they created a detailed plan for keeping the President safe through his visit and commencement speech.

On graduation day, there were barriers set-up and security checkpoints along the way heading into the assembly center where the graduation was held. These barriers and rules were in place to keep the President and all of the attendees safe. As President Bush arrived, there was a safety barrier between him and any crowds, and I would imagine that if a well-intentioned and enthusiastic fan of the President had jumped the barrier in order to get to the President, the fan would have been met with the harsh reality of a hard takedown and drawn weapons pointed in his direction. The barriers were there to set the appropriate boundaries for interacting with the President. The barriers were there to protect the nation's interests over the interests and desires of any individuals, even those with good intentions in their hearts towards the President. Boundaries are important. They protect, and this is true in true worship as well.

In his classical book *Worship: Old & New*, Robert Webber defined worship "in its broadest sense as a 'meeting between God and his people.'"[1] While this definition alone does not give us much clarity on what worship is, Webber obviously used this definition as a foundation to build on. He pointed to this "meeting between God and his people" as being a time of revelation and response. He argued that in worship, "God becomes present to his people, who respond with praise and thanksgiving."[2] Samuel Parkison, in his book *Revelation and Response*, argued that this pattern is the very essence or foundation of worship.

> Worship is comprised of two essential elements: Revelation and response. *Revelation* gives us the motivation to worship, and *response* is the expression of our worship.[3]

The question is, what does it look like to respond to God in acceptable worship? How is praise and thanksgiving properly expressed by a worshiper of the one, true God? Are there boundaries for the ways that we express our worship to God?

Starting in this chapter, we'll focus on the expressions of worship that are laid out for us in Scripture. As we begin to consider specific expressions of worship though, we must continually remember that worship starts and ends in the heart. Worship is -- most basically -- an expression of our position before the Lord and our heart's response to the Lord, but the Lord is a holy and righteous God!

---

[1] Robert Webber, *Worship old & new: A biblical, historical, and practical introduction* (Grand Rapids: Zondervan, 1982), 11.
[2] Ibid., 11-12.
[3] Samuel G. Parkison, *Revelation and Response: The Why and How of Leading Corporate Worship Through Song* (Spring Hill, TN: Rainer, 2018), 27.

There are boundaries that have been set-up to help us appropriately approach him. Yes, the boundaries have changed. By God's grace, the boundaries are different now than what they were in Genesis to Leviticus, but there are still boundaries. Plans and guidelines to shape the way we address and approach the Lord when we gather to worship him. So let's begin the journey of exploring some ways that worship is expressed in the Bible.

The First Sacrifice

After the sin of Adam and Eve in Genesis 3, death entered into the world through the first animal that was killed. The animal was sacrificed as a result of the sin of Adam and Eve, and the Lord used the skin of the animal to cover — literally and symbolically — the sin of Adam and Eve: "And the LORD God made for Adam and for his wife garments of skins and clothed them."[4] They were naked. They had always been naked, but for the first time, they were ashamed. The animal skin covered their nakedness; it covered their shame.

From this point forward, sacrifice in response to sin continued to be practiced by God's people; however, it wasn't until the Mosaic covenant that the various laws were established for the formal, sacrificial system for Israel's worship. In Leviticus 1-7, the Lord gave instructions for the various offerings and sacrifices that were provided as acceptable worship for his people. Of the five types of offerings and sacrifices, three were specifically connected to sin (the burnt offering, the sin offering, and the guilt offering). What became clear from Genesis 3 to the giving of the law was that the penalty for sin was death and that the shedding of blood was required for

---

[4] Gen. 3:21.

forgiveness. Both of these truths are explicitly stated in the New Testament as well.[5]

What's also clear was that the sacrifices in the Old Testament were never sufficient to remove the sins of God's people. Sacrifices and offerings were continually offered, over-and-over again, which pointed to the need for a better sacrifice. The sacrificial system revealed the hopeless sinfulness of man and cried out for a Savior to save man from his sin.

Sacrifice was an early expression of worship. It was a specific type of offering that was connected to atonement for sin, and in the Old Testament, sacrifices were a constant reminder of sin and the need for forgiveness, which we're reminded of in the New Testament book of Hebrews.

> For since the law has but a shadow of the good things to come instead of the true form of these realities, it can never, by the same sacrifices that are continually offered every year, make perfect those who draw near. Otherwise, would they not have ceased to be offered, since the worshipers, having once been cleansed, would no longer have any consciousness of sins? But in these sacrifices there is a reminder of sins every year. For it is impossible for the blood of bulls and goats to take away sins.[6]

Jesus was the spotless, sinless sacrificial Lamb of God who died for the sins of God's people! His sacrifice was once and for all. His

---

[5] Rom. 6:23; Heb. 9:22.
[6] Heb. 10:1-4.

sacrifice was final and complete, sufficiently atoning for the sin's of God's people and bringing complete and lasting forgiveness to those who put their faith in him, perfecting "for all time" those who believe.[7] Jesus' sacrifice was the final sacrifice that brought full forgiveness to those who believe.

> And by that will we have been sanctified through the offering of the body of Jesus Christ once for all.[8]

> And every priest stands daily at his service, offering the same sacrifices, which can never take away sin. But when Christ had offered for all time a single sacrifice for sins, he sat down at the right hand of God, waiting from that time until his enemies should be made a footstool for his feet. For by a single offering he has perfected for all time those who are being sanctified.[9]

Sacrifices were an integral part of worship in the history of worship. The sacrifice was an expression of confession and repentance. In the very act of sacrifice, sins were confessed, forgiveness was sought, thanksgiving was offered, and in all of this, sacrifice was an expression of worship that had been instituted by God himself. But you may say, "why?" What's the big deal, and why would sin require the death of these animals? Sacrifices are a foreign concept to most of us, which is only the result of the grace of God through the sacrifice of his Son Jesus on the cross, but sacrifices played an

---

[7] Heb. 10:14.
[8] Heb. 10:10.
[9] Heb. 10:11-14.

important role in revealing the significance of sin.[10] Sin's significance is found in the significance of the one we sin against.

Let's think back to President Bush attending my graduation. Imagine if someone had made it to the President with ill intentions. They yelled threats at him and were actually close enough to slap him in the face. Do you think the significance of their offense would be different than if they had yelled threats at me and slapped me in the face? The answer to that question is an easy "yes!" The one who threatened and slapped the President would have the secret service's and the attorney general's attention. Perhaps they would be looking at federal charges and swifter justice. Why? The significance of the offense changed because of the significance of the one they offended.

We have all sinned against the holy, Creator God of the universe, and we deserve the death penalty for our sin. Sin is significant because of the significance of the one we've sinned against. God in his grace, however, sent his Son to die for our sins. Praise God for the sacrifice of Jesus that put an end to animal sacrifices as an expression of our worship today.

Offering and Sacrifice

Immediately following the first sacrifice in connection to the sin of Adam and Eve, the sons of Adam and Eve are seen worshiping God through sacrifice and offerings.[11] Cain brought an offering from the produce of his field, and Abel brought an offering through the sacrifice of the first and best of his flock. In both cases, what we

---

[10] Rom. 7:7.
[11] Gen. 4:1-8.

learn is that sacrifice and offering was always intended to be a responsive act of worship. Cain and Abel were supposed to be responding to what God had given them through the act of giving back to God through the sacrifice and offering, which acknowledged and thanked the Lord for his provision and displayed faith in his future provision. This responsive nature of worship is quickly seen again in the life of Noah.

When God delivered Noah and his family through the flood, the first thing that Noah did when he exited the Ark onto dry ground was to take some of the precious few animals from the Ark and to sacrifice them to the Lord.[12] It was an extravagant sacrifice and offering that matched the extravagant grace of God in his salvation of the animals and Noah's family through the flood. Finally, the most common Hebrew word for worship is used in the Old Testament in connection to Abraham's obedience in taking his only son Isaac to be sacrificed to the Lord.[13] In this incredible response to the Lord, Abraham displayed his faith in God and his trust in God's promise for his son's future, despite the seemingly contradictory command to sacrifice his only son. In all of these examples, we see that true worship in sacrifice and offering came from hearts that were responding in gratefulness and obedience to the Lord.

As I write these words, still thinking about Abraham with Isaac on that altar on the mountain, I'm thinking about my children and my grandchild. When my granddaughter was eight-months-old, she was too young to talk or to draw me a picture, but she was already starting to try to give me things. One night, we were at a noodle restaurant with our family, and I was holding my granddaughter. She had a

---

[12] Gen. 8:20.
[13] Gen. 22:5.

noodle spoon that she was playing with and dropping on the floor (I think our waitress brought our granddaughter at least three spoons that night!). At one point, my granddaughter looked at me intently, and she extended her spoon to my mouth. My heart was full of joy, knowing that she was trying to share with her Pawpaw!

My granddaughter's gift had no financial value, but it was relationally priceless. At the same time, I've received gifts from others that did have financial value, but they were given with strings attached. In my career before I surrendered to gospel ministry, the employees who worked in my area would often give me gifts for Christmas or Boss's Day. Vendors would even give us swag or treat us to dinner at times. While some of these gifts came from genuine friendship or genuine gratitude, I do know that some of these gifts also came with ulterior motives. Perhaps the motive was financial, hoping that we'd buy their product or that I'd recommend them for a raise. Perhaps the motive was relational, hoping that I'd feel some sense of obligation or relational commitment to them. I don't know for sure what their motives were, but I know for sure that some gifts were given for selfish motives. You can tell, right?

I'm certain that God can tell too. True worship in sacrifice and offering comes from hearts that are responding in gratefulness and obedience to the Lord. Today, while sacrifices are no longer needed for our sin, the Lord still deserves our offerings in response to what he's given and done, and in that, God deserves the very first and best of what he has given us in life. Is your worship responsive? Are you giving the Lord the very first and best of what he's given you? Do you see and realize that all you have comes from him?

Acceptable Offerings and Sacrifices

In these early pictures of sacrifice and offering, the Lord gives us important insight into what makes a sacrifice or offering acceptable. In the case of Cain and Abel, there's little explicit explanation of what made Abel's offering acceptable and what made Cain's unacceptable, but there is an implicit explanation given in the text, which points to two critical things. First, while Abel gave from the first and the very best of his flock, Cain simply gave from the produce of his field. There seems to be an implication that while Abel's offering required real sacrifice and displayed real faith and gratefulness, Cain's did not. Secondly -- and perhaps more importantly -- what follows gives us clarity into the heart of Cain. Immediately, jealousy and hate filled Cain's heart.

> . . . And the LORD had regard for Abel and his offering, but for Cain and his offering he had no regard. So Cain was very angry, and his face fell. The LORD said to Cain, "Why are you angry, and why has your face fallen? If you do well, will you not be accepted? And if you do not do well, sin is crouching at the door. Its desire is contrary to you, but you must rule over it."[14]

Cain's concern was more for his brother than for the Lord. The first problem related to his offering was connected to the more primary problem of his heart in worship.

In the case of Abraham, when God stopped Abraham from sacrificing his son Isaac, the Lord declared, ". . . now I know that

---

[14] Gen. 4:4-7.

you fear God, seeing you have not withheld your son, your only son, from me."[15] In other words, the heart of the act was what mattered most to the Lord. The act of sacrificing his son Isaac would not have been pleasing to God.

During the time of the prophets, the Lord clearly articulated this truth through the prophet Isaiah when he told the people that their sacrifices and offerings were meaningless without hearts of true repentance and obedience,[16] and in the New Testament, Jesus emphasized this same truth, expounding in various ways on the truth that for an offering to be acceptable to the Lord, the heart of the one making the offering must be acceptable to the Lord. Therefore, he taught that if you had something against your brother, you needed to go and be reconciled with your brother before you brought your offering to the Lord.[17] He also taught that it wasn't the amount of the offering that made the offering significant; rather, it was the true sacrifice and faith in the heart of the giver that made the offering significant to the Lord.[18]

Your heart matters most in what you give to the Lord. You must be right with the Lord to give rightly to the Lord. God doesn't want our offerings if they come with lots of strings and expectations attached to them. It's not worship if it's considered a quid pro quo: I'll do this for you, if you'll do this for me. True worship in offering comes from a heart with no strings attached; however, we do know that there is blessing that comes through true offering. The apostle Paul captures

---

[15] Gen. 22:12.
[16] Isa. 1:10-17.
[17] Matt. 5:21-24.
[18] Mark 12:41-44.

all of these truths in his words of encouragement for grace-driven giving to the church in Corinth:

> So I thought it necessary to urge the brothers to go on ahead to you and arrange in advance for the gift that you have promised, so that it may be ready as a willing gift, not as an exaction. The point is this: whoever sows sparingly will also reap sparingly, and whoever sows bountifully will also reap bountifully. Each one of you must give as he has decided in his heart, not reluctantly or under compulsion, for God loves a cheerful giver. And God is able to make all grace abound to you, so that having all sufficiency in all things at all times, you may abound in every good work. As it is written, "He has distributed freely, he has given to the poor; his righteousness endures forever." He who supplies seed to the sower and bread for food will supply and multiply your seed for sowing and increase the harvest of your righteousness. You will be enriched in every way to be generous in every way, which through us will produce thanksgiving to God.[19]

Paul was reminding the Corinthian believers that they needed to regularly and willingly set aside the offerings that they promised to give for the work of God.[20] He also reminded them in a beautiful way that investments in the work of God will pay dividends in the work of God.[21] Unlike the snake-oil selling "evangelist" on

---

[19] 2 Cor. 9:5-11.
[20] 2 Cor. 9:1-5.
[21] 2 Cor. 9:6.

television, Paul wasn't requesting a seed gift of $1,000 so that the giver would get a return gift of $10,000 from the Lord. This reality is clear from the dividends that Paul made clear in this passage, which included (1) growth in righteousness in the life of the giver; (2) meeting the needs of the saints; and (3) bringing thanksgiving to God through the needs that were met through the offering that was given.[22]

Through the apostle Paul, the Lord provided a litmus test for our hearts when it comes to worship through giving from our pocketbooks. The list is all found in one verse: 2 Corinthians 9:7, and it's worth not only reviewing the litmus test but also using the litmus test to assess our hearts when it comes to worship in the offerings we give. Read 2 Corinthians 9:7 below, and then use this litmus test to review your heart of worship through your financial offerings to the Lord: "Each one of you must give as he has decided in his heart, not reluctantly or under compulsion, for God loves a cheerful giver."

Are these things a part of your offerings to the Lord?

> (1) You should give to God as he leads you in your heart to give.
>
> (2) You should give to God because you want to give to the Lord.
>
> (3) You should give to God cheerfully because you want to please the Lord.

---

[22] 2 Cor. 9:8-15.

When it comes to worship through giving to the Lord, are your offerings acceptable? Did you pass the litmus test? It's important to remember, though, that offering and sacrifice today in our worship isn't restricted to our financial gifts alone. There's more we're called to give.

The Sacrifice We're Still Called to Give

Consider all we've been given in Christ: The temple, the priesthood, and the sacrifices have all been fulfilled in Jesus. We have God's presence with us. We are a priesthood of believers, and there's no need for animal sacrifices anymore. We have been justified by faith in Jesus through his atoning death on the cross for our sins. We have been raised to a new and forgiven life in Christ through the victory and the power of the resurrection. So how do we respond to this incredible gift of new and forgiven life that God has given us? The only reasonable way for us to respond is to worship. How? In part by giving ourselves to the Lord.

While there is no longer a need for the sacrifice of bulls and goats, there is a call for a living sacrifice to be made. We are called to be living sacrifices, which is only doing what is reasonable.[23] The Lord calls us to give our lives as living sacrifices, offered to the Lord who gave us life, and this is where offerings and sacrifice still come together.

Our offerings are not only monetary — although they are not less than monetary — but our offerings to the Lord include everything we have to give, from our praise and finances to our very lives! Listen to what Paul said to his beloved brothers and sisters in the Philippian

---

[23] Rom. 12:1-2.

church, "Even if I am to be poured out as a drink offering upon the sacrificial offering of your faith, I am glad and rejoice with you all."[24]

In putting on the glasses of God's Word, take a few minutes to prayerfully reflect on this chapter, and then ask for the Lord's wisdom and discernment as you answer the questions below about what offering and sacrifice look like in your life and in your church.

Applying God's Truth

(1) What does offering and sacrifice look like in your life?

(2) What does offering and sacrifice look like when you gather as the church?

(3) Are you offering to God what is right and reasonable based on all that he's given you?

---

[24] Phil. 2:17.

(4) Are your offerings to God responsive and routine? Why? Does anything need to change?

(5) What has the Lord convicted you of today? What do you need to do to take steps in keeping with repentance in your life?

Chapter 3:

Prayer

"I'm guilty, your honor." Have you ever stood before a judge and said those words? I have -- one time long ago. I received a speeding ticket for going about 7 miles over the speed limit. It was a speed trap that was set up right at the foot of a bridge, and to make matters worse, it was Father's Day. I was just coming back from a short fishing trip that went about as well as my drive home. I was guilty, but the officer who gave me the ticket also gave me a way to wash my speeding ticket away. He told me that if I went to court and pled guilty, the judge would change my ticket to a non-moving violation, which sounded like good news to me. I decided the effort was worth the reward, so I spent a morning sitting in a courtroom, waiting for my turn to stand before the judge and say "I'm guilty."

When my name was finally called, enabling me to stand before the judge, one of the first things I had to do was address him. I had heard it on T.V. and in court that morning, but it felt a little strange coming from my mouth: "Your honor" is what I said. That's a title of respect and recognition. "Your honor" recognizes the position and authority of the judge, and it shows the proper respect and understanding of my corresponding position before the judge. Before I could present my guilt and ask for his mercy, I had to recognize who he was in order to rightly relate to him. This is obvious, and it's appropriate. I think it also points towards something that's a good starting point when it comes to prayer: In prayer, God's people worship God through hearts that call on the name of the Lord.

Who We Pray To

In Genesis 4, God provided a picture of how sinfulness was unfolding and increasing in the world. From the first murder that occurred when Cain killed his brother Abel, to the boastful sin of Lamech, who was one of Cain's descendents, life on earth was marked by the sinfulness of man. At the end of the chapter, however, we see a glimmer of hope in these words: "At that time people began to call on the name of the Lord."[1] In this elementary statement, we are pointed to an expression of worship that connects most basically to the heart of worship. People began to call on the name of the Lord, recognizing him for who he is: Their Creator and their hope to deliver them from sin and the effects of sin in the world.

While this "calling on the name of the Lord" may point to broader expressions of worship, it clearly points to the heart of true prayer. As God's people began silently and verbally calling out to the Lord, his people began to pray. Throughout Scripture, the prayers of God's people started with the recognition and identification of the recipient of their prayers. Prayer starts with recognizing who God is and also recognizing our corresponding position before him. Here are just a few examples that are repeated throughout the pages of the Bible. Note the recognition of the Lord in these verses from the mouths of those praying to the Lord.

As Moses recounted his journey with God's people to the edge of the Promised Land, he recalled the following:

> And I prayed to the LORD, "O Lord GOD, do not destroy your people and your heritage, whom you

---

[1] Gen. 4:26b.

> have redeemed through your greatness, whom you have brought out of Egypt with a mighty hand . ."[2]

When Elisha prayed for his servants eyes to be opened so that he could see the Lord's provision, he called to the Lord:

> Then Elisha prayed and said, "O LORD, please open his eyes that he may see." So the LORD opened the eyes of the young man, and he saw, and behold, the mountain was full of horses and chariots of fire all around Elisha."[3]

This pattern continued into the New Testament period as seen in the early church as they gathered together in a time of crisis to call to the Lord:

> And when they heard it, they lifted their voices together to God and said, "Sovereign Lord, who made the heaven and the earth and the sea and everything in them . . ."[4]

And Jesus provided the simple yet profound example of prayer for us when he taught us to pray like this:

> Pray then like this: "Our Father in heaven, hallowed be your name."[5]

---

[2] Deut. 9:26.
[3] 2 Kings 6:17.
[4] Acts 4:24.
[5] Matt. 6:9.

In these examples and so many more in Scripture, God's people prayed to the Lord, who is the Sovereign God and who is our Heavenly Father by his grace to us through Jesus his Son. From the example of God's people to the instruction of Jesus, it's clear that biblical prayer begins with the recognition and identification of the Lord. The Lord is who we look to and who we call on in prayer, and in that reality, prayer is a beautiful confession and expression of a heart that is looking to and calling on the Lord. Prayer is worship because it is a response to the revelation that God is the one we need to call on in our lives.

Another thing that we see consistently in God's Word is that prayer is a part of both personal and corporate worship. As people began to call on the name of the Lord in Genesis 4, they were calling out to the Lord both personally and collectively. Elisha prayed privately to the Lord for his servant's eyes to be open so he could see the army of angels that surrounded them and defended them, and the early church in Acts 4 prayed corporately to the Lord that he would empower them and embolden them to continue to speak the gospel in the face of growing opposition and persecution. In all cases, though, their prayers began with a recognition of the Lord.

That's appropriate, isn't it? That should be the starting place that frames our communication with God. Like standing before the judge in that courtroom, it's essential that we know who we are talking to and that we approach the Lord from a position of recognition and respect for who he is: His position, his power, his authority, and his grace. But what are the things that lead us to call on the Lord?

What We Pray For

As the prayers of God's people are expressed throughout the pages of Scripture, it is clear that there is repetition in the subject matter of prayer. This shouldn't be surprising. All disaster, sickness, danger, difficulty, death, etc. exists in the world because of sin. People from every generation and every geographic location face the same fundamental issues of sin and the same consequences of sin in life. Therefore, some of the earliest examples of God's people praying were for the confession of sin. When the conviction of sin occurs in one's heart, the only acceptable response is to call on the name of the Lord, who has the power to forgive sin. This is seen in God's people from the Old Testament to the New Testament, and the Lord Jesus taught us to consistently pray for the forgiveness of sin as we extend forgiveness to others for their sins that impact our lives.[6]

Consider these examples of prayer that confess sin and look to the Lord for forgiveness:

> And the people came to Moses and said, "We have sinned, for we have spoken against the LORD and against you. Pray to the LORD, that he take away the serpents from us." So Moses prayed for the people.[7]

> While Ezra prayed and made confession, weeping and casting himself down before the house of God, a very great assembly of men, women, and children,

---

[6] Matt. 6:12.
[7] Num. 21:7.

> gathered to him out of Israel, for the people wept bitterly.[8]

> . . . and forgive us our debts, as we also have forgiven our debtors.[9]

> Therefore, confess your sins to one another and pray for one another, that you may be healed. The prayer of a righteous person has great power as it is working.[10]

While prayer can certainly be private as well as corporate, notice that all of these examples of prayer are in connection with the confession of sin and the seeking of forgiveness within the context of corporate prayer. Moses prayed for the people in response to their confession of sin and their request for Moses to seek the Lord on their behalf. Ezra publicly mourned and confessed sin to the Lord, which the Lord used to lead many others to join their repentant hearts together with Ezra before the Lord. Jesus taught us to pray by giving us a model prayer that was meant to be prayed with others: "Us," "our," and "we" can only be understood within the context of a group of believers and not just an individual believer praying for himself. In James 5:16, God calls you to "confess your sins one to another and pray for one another."

Another frequent theme in prayer is the cry or plea for deliverance. In this fallen, sinful world, God's people have always been faced with persecution, hate, and danger. In a real way, in the midst of these threats to life, believers call on the name of the Lord. More

---

[8] Ezra 10:1.
[9] Matt. 6:12.
[10] Jas. 5:16.

importantly, though, than just the temporal deliverance from danger in this life is the eternal deliverance of the danger of hell. The church is called on to pray for God's work of salvation in the lives of the lost in the world. We're given the gift of being able to pray for deliverance in this world.

The Psalms are a common place for prayers of deliverance and salvation. As God's people faced their enemies and the consequences of their own sin, they cried to the Lord for the deliverance that only he could provide. From the time of the united kingdom to the exile and return, the Psalms remind us that God is the one we should call on for deliverance and salvation in this life. Consider these desperate calls for deliverance from the Psalms.

> Answer me when I call, O God of my righteousness! You have given me relief when I was in distress. Be gracious to me and hear my prayer![11]
>
> Oh, guard my soul, and deliver me! Let me not be put to shame, for I take refuge in you.[12]
>
> Deliver me from all my transgressions. Do not make me the scorn of the fool![13]
>
> Vindicate me, O God, and defend my cause against an ungodly people, from the deceitful and unjust man deliver me![14]

---

[11] Psa. 4:1.
[12] Psa. 25:20.
[13] Psa. 39:8.
[14] Psa. 43:1.

It's worth taking time to search for passages in the Psalms that ask for the Lord's deliverance and salvation. There are many, and they remind us of the many things we need deliverance from in this life, from the physical, to the social, and to the spiritual. In the New Testament, Jesus validated this beautiful gift of being able to go to the Lord for deliverance. In his model prayer, he taught us to pray for deliverance like this: "And lead us not into temptation, but deliver us from evil."[15]

The early church put the example of their Old Testament brothers and the words of their Lord to practice. When Peter was in prison in Jerusalem, here's what the early church did: "So Peter was kept in prison, but earnest prayer for him was made to God by the church."[16] When the apostle Paul was in chains with an uncertain future, he joyfully wrote these words to his brothers and sisters in Philippi: ". . . for I know that through your prayers and the help of the Spirit of Jesus Christ this will turn out for my deliverance."[17] And when Paul wrote to the church in Rome, who he longed to meet, he revealed the intimate desire of his heart towards the lost when he said, "Brothers, my heart's desire and prayer to God for them is that they may be saved."[18]

Yet another common expression of prayer in Scripture is for provision in life. These supplications range from the gift of a baby,[19] to spiritual insight,[20] to physical protection,[21] to ordaining and

---

[15] Matt. 6:13.
[16] Acts 12:5.
[17] Phil. 1:19.
[18] Rom. 10:1.
[19] 1 Sam. 1:10.
[20] 2 Kgs. 6:17.
[21] Neh. 4:9.

blessing God's call on his servants,[22] to healing,[23] and anything else! When in need, God's people go to God no matter how big or how small, and perhaps most importantly, the prayers of God's people are often mixed with praise and thanksgiving to God. When Hannah's prayer for a baby was answered, she responded: "And Hannah prayed and spoke these words, 'My heart exults in the LORD; my horn is exalted in the LORD. My mouth derides my enemies, because I rejoice in your salvation.'"[24] In fact, we are commanded to offer our prayers with thanksgiving!

> Do not be anxious about anything, but in everything by prayer and supplication with thanksgiving let your requests be made known to God.[25]
>
> Continue steadfastly in prayer, being watchful in it with thanksgiving.[26]

What does all of this mean? Collectively, God's Word makes it clear that God's people express their dependence on God and need for God through prayer. This position of dependence is a position of worship, looking to God to provide what we need in life. In looking at prayer in Scripture, I'm reminded that prayer is such a fundamental expression of worship for God's people. Today, however, it seems to be relegated to such an insignificant or perfunctory role in a lot of the worship of God's people. Let me ask you a question: Does prayer in your church look like the prayer that

---

[22] Acts 13:3.
[23] Jas. 5:13-14.
[24] 1 Sam. 2:1.
[25] Phil. 4:6.
[26] Col. 4:2.

we've briefly explored in God's Word? It should, and by God's grace, I pray that it will. God hasn't left us without a roadmap for growing prayer in our churches. He's given us all we need to allow him to help our churches become devoted to prayer.

How We Must Pray

While there are examples of individual believers praying directly to God in the Old Testament, the majority of written prayers in the Old Testament are voiced by God's leaders. Many times, God's people asked their leader to pray to God on their behalf. In the New Testament, something beautiful occurs. Jesus taught his disciples to pray, and he urged them to pray persistently through both his example of consistent prayer and his teaching on prayer. As the early church was born after the resurrection and ascension of Jesus Christ, the church as a whole was marked by prayer! They devoted themselves to prayer as they waited on the promise of the Holy Spirit, and they continued to devote themselves to prayer as they lived in the abundance of the Spirit. The church was given clear instructions and commands related to prayer, including the following:

- Pray together,[27]
- Pray constantly,[28]
- Pray about everything,[29] and
- Pray with thanksgiving.[30]

---

[27] Acts 1:14; 2:42.
[28] Rom. 12:12; Eph 6:18; Col. 4:2; 1 Thes. 5:17.
[29] Phil. 4:6.
[30] Phil. 4:6; Col. 4:2.

Let's take a minute to examine each of these directives on prayer. First, the church must pray together. This seems so basic that perhaps you may think it should go without saying. I agree; it should! However, the state of prayer in many churches and in many worship services would suggest otherwise. It needs to be stated, over-and-over again. We need to be reminded of the priority and the importance of prayer for the church, as seen in the priority and use of prayer in the church in Scripture.

Let me ask you a question, what does prayer look like in your worship services? For some, there may be written prayers that are read as part of the service for that day. For others, there may be the standard opening and closing prayer and maybe a prayer for the offering. For a few, perhaps there are pastoral prayers during the service for specific things in the church, in the community, or in the world. Most of these prayers, however, are prayers offered by one person, who is praying for the church or perhaps on behalf of the church. Church members can listen and join in with prayerful agreement to what is prayed, and when this happens, the church is praying together. But do they participate in prayer, or do they just listen (or daydream)? Surely, some do join in prayer, but is that encouraged? Is it taught? Is it welcomed? Congregational engagement and participation in prayer is a critical part of worship, which requires teaching and leadership to cultivate and to grow an understanding and a heart for prayer in a congregation.

Second, the church is commanded to pray constantly. Obviously, this command points to a heart that is continually depending on, recognizing, and calling on the Lord. It's a prayerful attitude in our lives for sure, but it also indicates that our lives should be marked by actual prayer on a very regular and constant basis. How do you do this? What does this look like practically? Let me try to give you some simple ways that this could play out in your private prayer and in your prayer with others.

I was recently in the book of Daniel, and I was reminded and convicted of prayer in my life when I read chapter 6. You know the story. The Babylonian empire had been conquered, and Darius the Mede was now in charge. Unknowingly, he's convinced to make a law that's intended to trap Daniel, and it does. The law prohibited any resident of the kingdom from praying to anyone other than the king for thirty days. When Daniel heard that the law had been signed, do you remember what he did? He went up to his room, just as he always did three times each day, and he got on his knees to pray in front of the window that was opened towards Jerusalem. Daniel prayed.

Daniel knew the risk. He knew the consequences of breaking the law, but faithfulness to God was what mattered most to Daniel. For Daniel, prayer was literally a matter of life or death. I think on a personal level, we need to see prayer for what it truly is: A matter of life or death. Without prayer, life in the Spirit can't live. Without prayer, we dry up spiritually. Prayer is the water and food that's needed for our life and growth in Christ. Prayer fuels our relationship and passion for the Lord, and it heals and renews our wearied souls. Prayer is what we need to live.

So personally, make prayer a matter of life or death. I've decided to follow Daniel's pattern of prayer for a season in my life, designating times of prayer throughout each day where everything else must wait and all of my attention must be on the Lord. While I want a constant attitude of prayer in my heart, I also need a consistent practice of prayer in my life. To pray constantly, prayer must be a consistent practice in our lives, and if it's not a matter of life or death, it won't be. Prayer will be pushed to the side, delayed, and eventually forsaken. So make prayer a consistent practice to pray constantly in your life.

I do believe, however, that praying with others is what really brings the meaning of "pray constantly" to life. If we have an attitude of prayer in our lives, there's actually an abundance of opportunities for prayer -- learning how to pray and teaching others to pray -- through the opportunities the Lord brings to us each and every day. In our church, I encourage our staff to pray with others as they talk to others. Praying immediately and responsively is a good practice to help us keep a heart of prayer and to grow in the practice of prayer. As we talk to others and discover their hurts, needs, opportunities, and joys, pray with them. Pray in the hallway, in the pew, in the store, on the street, in the kitchen, and in the parking lot. This is another way that our personal prayer is encouraged and grown, when we open up to begin praying with others about whatever is going on in our lives.

Corporately, I long for deeper and more engaged prayer as the church gathers in worship. The church needs believers praying together in worship just as we sing together, listen to God's Word together, and share in the Lord's Supper together. Traditionally, one way corporate prayer has been accomplished in worship is through the reciting of prayers, especially the Lord's Prayer within Christian worship. This comes out of the tradition of first century synagogue worship, when the prayers were a regular part of the gathering of faithful Jews in worship. In the synagogue, recited prayers such as the *Yotzer*, *Ahabah*, and the *Shema* provided familiar prayers, full of biblical and doctrinal truth, that allowed worshipers to participate in worship through prayer when gathered together.[31] While reciting prayers can be beneficial for leading the church to pray together, this still seems to fall short of the type of "praying together" that is seen in the early church in the book of Acts. What is still needed are times of leading and allowing the church to pray together, turning their hearts responsively and immediately to call on the name of the Lord in connection to the things in their lives, their church, their community, and the world.

Third, the church can pray about everything. There's nothing too small or too large to bring to God in prayer. In everything in our lives and in the church, we should pray. This is good news, isn't it? I think back, years ago, to when my grandfather on my mother's side passed away, leaving his house and belongings to my mother and her brother. My grandparents had quite a few cats that lived under the house. My grandmother was the only one who could touch most of the cats, so once my grandfather died, there was a problem: What were we going to do with the cats? My mother knew what to do. She prayed. She's a prayer warrior anyway. She knew that if there wasn't anyone else who cared about the cats and could find a home for the cats, God did, and God could. Guess what? God did!

Think back to the idea of praying with others. The reality that we are invited to pray about everything opens up the opportunity for prayer with others in an extraordinary way. From the youngest to the oldest, we can pray together because we can pray about everything. From the mundane to the life-changing, we can pray about it because we can pray about anything. As we gather to worship, we have an

---

[31] Horton Davies, *Christian Worship: Its Making and Meaning* (Wallington: The Religious Education Press, 1957), 17-18.

opportunity to teach and to engage the church in prayer because we can pray about everything.

Finally, the church should pray with thanksgiving. This instruction is a gift from God, as reminding and recounting the things that we have to be thankful for is medicine to the broken-hearted and hope to the spirit struggling with hopelessness. Thankfulness is the right heart condition of the worshiper before God. When we know the Creator, there's a reason to be thankful for every minute of life we've been given. When we know the Provider, there's a reason to be thankful for every blessing of provision we've received. When we know the Comforter, there's a reason to be thankful for every mercy we've been shown. When we know the Defender, there's a reason to be thankful for every protection we've been provided. When we know the Redeemer, there's a reason to be thankful for every forgiven sin and for every minute of eternity we've been promised. Because prayer is worship that is so closely connected to the heart of worship, the church should devote itself to prayer.

Encouragement to Pray

In the book of Revelation, we're given a glimpse into heaven and given an illustration of how the prayers of God's people are received by God in heaven. The picture is of an altar of incense, with the sweet-smelling smoke of the incense rising up to the Lord with the prayers of God's people. In other words, the prayers of the saints — those who are called and set-apart by God through his grace in Jesus Christ — are like a fragrant offering to the Lord. They are acceptable and are received by God.

> And when he had taken the scroll, the four living creatures and the twenty-four elders fell down

> before the Lamb, each holding a harp, and golden bowls full of incense, which are the prayers of the saints.[32]

> And another angel came and stood at the altar with a golden censer, and he was given much incense to offer with the prayers of all the saints on the golden altar before the throne, and the smoke of the incense, with the prayers of the saints, rose before God from the hand of the angel.[33]

There's no clearer picture in all of Scripture that shows us that prayer is worship. The prayers of God's church are a sweet offering to the Lord. Why? Perhaps fatherhood can give us a glimpse into one important reason why. My wife and I entered the empty nester stage a few years ago. However, even though our children are grown and on their own, we still love to hear from our children. In fact, I received a text message from one of our children as I was writing this chapter. The message was short and simple. My daughter was just checking to see how I was feeling today because I was sick last week. She told me that she loved me and that she was looking forward to seeing me over the coming weekend. Her text made me smile. When I get a text or call from our adult children, it makes me happy. I love to know that they still think about me -- regardless of the reason -- and I still enjoy hearing from them when they reach out to me.

As God's children, adopted into his family by his grace through faith in Jesus Christ, we have the privilege and opportunity to approach

---

[32] Rev. 5:8.
[33] Rev. 8:3-4.

the throne of God and to lift our voices in confidence, calling to our Heavenly Father through prayer. The incredible thing is that the prayers of God's children are like a sweet offering to the Lord. What a joy and privilege we have in prayer! Prayer must not be just a prelude or a postlude to worship. Prayer must be an integral part of the worship of God in our lives throughout the week and as we gather with our church to worship.

Let's take a minute to prayerfully apply this chapter to our lives and to our churches. Use the questions below to reflect on prayer. Perhaps make a prayer list to begin using daily in your prayer and weekly with your church.

Applying God's Truth

> (1) How do you recognize and acknowledge God in prayer? Why is this important? How does the way we call on God reveal what we think about God?

> (2) To confess basically means to agree with. With that in mind, what does it mean to confess our sins? Are there any sins that you need to confess right now?

> (3) Read the passages connected to prayer in Acts 1 and 2. Is this what prayer looks like in your life? What about in

your church? If not, how can you cultivate this kind of prayer?

(4) When you gather for worship with your church, what does prayer look like in your worship service? What's good about your worship in prayer? Are there any issues with prayer in your worship services? What are some practical ways that your church can pray together when you come together to worship?

Chapter 4:
Praise

Do you ever feel like singing? Even if you can't hold a tune, you've probably felt the urge to belt out the words of a song at some point in your life. This probably happens in your car or truck with the radio blasting and where no other ears can hear. All of us enjoy some type of music. All of us love to hear a good song and to listen to someone who can sing. All of us have a desire or urge to sing from time to time. Why is that? We have a desire to sing because God's given us the capacity to sing. When it comes to worship, singing is a wonderful gift that should be a part of our worship of God, and just as with prayer, praise in song is worship only when it comes from a heart of worship.

So if singing is a gift from God that's intended for our worship of God, how do we see this truth affirmed and informed in God's Word? Let's take a minute to explore what Scripture has to say about praise through song, but first, let's address the obvious elephant in the room when it comes to music in worship: The worship wars.

Years ago, an old family friend jokingly told me that "when Satan was cast out of heaven, he fell right down into the choir loft." At the time, I appreciated the sentiment. I had been asked to play the acoustic guitar to help accompany the choir with a new song they were leading one Sunday. Apparently, this was the first time that a guitar had ever been played during a Sunday morning worship service at this church. I was unaware of that, but I wasn't unaware of what happened after the song was played. There were vocal complaints, and there were written complaints, including one that was typed, cut, and pasted like a serial killer's note. The fall out was emotional and hurtful, but it was also illogical to me. What was the basis for such an impassioned and borderline psychotic response? Where in Scripture was a stringed guitar associated with Satan and forbidden in worship? I wanted a logical reason for the reaction, but there wasn't one. The response to the guitar being played in church wasn't logical. It was emotional. It wasn't grounded in theology. It is deeply rooted in personal preferences. That was one of my first encounters with what some call "the worship wars." I now understood why it was called a war.

In my years of experience in the church, music seems to be the one thing that consistently has the ability to stir up division and disagreement. Like the temperature of the porridge in *Goldilocks and the Three Little Bears*, we all have our preferences on what makes music just right, which means that the music is rarely just right for everyone in the church. Week-to-week, the music is probably too loud for some and not loud enough for others. The instruments are too old-school for this group and too contemporary for that group. The songs are too old and too long for these folks and too new and too repetitive for those folks. We could keep going, couldn't we? The point is that what we like related to music is most often driven by preferences and not by theology. Sure, many -- hopefully most -- are interested in songs that are Scripturally-rich and theologically-accurate, but ultimately, what drives whether someone likes a song or not is preference. Honestly, I hope to change that in some hearts. I hope that this chapter will help us all look at praise in song through the lens of Scripture, approaching music in worship more from theology than preference. I think some of us will be surprised when we do, so in this chapter, my goal is to explore what God's Word clearly reveals about worship through music. From examples of singing to commands about singing, let's allow God's Word to speak and to shape our hearts for worship through song.

Sing!

The first recorded pictures of worship through singing are beautiful moments in history where God's people naturally and joyfully proclaimed their praise to God through song, declaring who God was and what God had done. In the first scene of responsive singing in the Bible, the Lord had led his people out of captivity in Egypt, bringing them through the Red Sea on dry ground. He then had powerfully destroyed Pharaoh and his army in the Red Sea as they pursued God's people, who were leaving Egypt. In response to this dramatic deliverance by God, Moses led the Israelites in singing a song of praise to the Lord, which recounted what God had done and ascribed to him the praise he deserved.

> Then Moses and the people of Israel sang this song to the LORD, saying, "I will sing to the LORD, for he has triumphed gloriously; the horse and his rider he has thrown into the sea. The LORD is my strength and my song, and he has become my salvation; this is my God, and I will praise him, my father's God, and I will exalt him."[1]

Miriam, who was the wife of Moses, even followed with leading the women in a song that called on God's people to sing in praise to the Lord.[2] This pattern continued even in the book of Judges, as

---

[1] Exod. 15:1-2.
[2] Exod. 15:21.

Deborah and Barak sang about God's deliverance of Israel from Jabin, the king of Canaan.

> Then sang Deborah and Barak the son of Abinoam on that day: "That the leaders took the lead in Israel, that the people offered themselves willingly, bless the LORD! "Hear, O kings; give ear, O princes; to the LORD I will sing; I will make melody to the LORD, the God of Israel.[3]

But it wasn't until the time of King David that the Lord began to formalize the role of singers in worship. David first appointed Levites to sing in their service at the tabernacle. David later organized the musicians among the Levites in their service in music.

> And they brought in the ark of God and set it inside the tent that David had pitched for it, and they offered burnt offerings and peace offerings before God. And when David had finished offering the burnt offerings and the peace offerings, he blessed the people in the name of the LORD and distributed to all Israel, both men and women, to each a loaf of bread, a portion of meat, and a cake of raisins. Then he appointed some of the Levites as ministers before the ark of the LORD, to invoke, to thank, and to praise the LORD, the God of Israel.[4]

---

[3] Judg. 5:1-3.
[4] 1 Chr. 16:1-4.

> Then on that day David first appointed that thanksgiving be sung to the LORD by Asaph and his brothers.[5]

> The number of them along with their brothers, who were trained in singing to the LORD, all who were skillful, was 288.[6]

In later years in the divided kingdom, singing in worship is often seen as an important part of the renewal of covenant worship under the reforming kings of Judah, including Jehosaphat in 2 Chronicles 20 and Hezekiah in 2 Chronicles 29:

> And when he had taken counsel with the people, he appointed those who were to sing to the LORD and praise him in holy attire, as they went before the army, and say, "Give thanks to the LORD, for his steadfast love endures forever."[7]

> The whole assembly worshiped, and the singers sang, and the trumpeters sounded. All this continued until the burnt offering was finished.[8]

Even after the exile, singing was witnessed among the returning and rebuilding period of time as the Jews began to return to Jerusalem to rebuild their city.

---

[5] 1 Chr. 16:7.
[6] 1 Chr. 25:7.
[7] 2 Chr. 20:21.
[8] 2 Chr. 29:28.

> And they sang responsively, praising and giving thanks to the LORD, "For he is good, for his steadfast love endures forever toward Israel." And all the people shouted with a great shout when they praised the LORD, because the foundation of the house of the LORD was laid.[9]

But perhaps the most compelling, biblical case for expressing praise in song is seen in the book of Psalms. This descriptive prayer book and songbook for God's people provides numerous examples of worship through the singing of praises. In fact, in the language of the Old Testament, there is a common word used in the book of Psalms that combines singing and praise. The single word, which translates "to sing praise," occurs 32 times in the book of Psalms. Sometimes the word occurs in describing what God's people do in response to what he has done, and oftentimes the word occurs to describe what God's people are called to do because of who God is and what God has done. Consider these few examples below:

> I will give to the LORD the thanks due to his righteousness, and I will sing praise to the name of the LORD, the Most High.[10]

> I will be glad and exult in you; I will sing praise to your name, O Most High.[11]

---

[9] Ezra 3:11-12.
[10] Psa. 7:17.
[11] Psa. 9:2.

> Sing praises to the LORD, who sits enthroned in Zion! Tell among the peoples his deeds![12]

> Sing praises to the LORD, O you his saints, and give thanks to his holy name.[13]

> . . . that my glory may sing your praise and not be silent. O LORD my God, I will give thanks to you forever![14]

> Sing praises to God, sing praises! Sing praises to our King, sing praises! For God is the King of all the earth; sing praises with a psalm![15]

All of this reveals the truth that singing is a common and consistent way that praise is expressed to God.

There's something else that's so important to recognize: Singing is an expression of worship in the hearts of God's people. Singing doesn't manufacture worship. This is an important distinction, because I think many are prone to see it the other way around. Many experience something they deem as worship when they are moved by the music, but can we trust our feelings? Does a feeling affirm worship? To help us think about these questions, let me give you a quick example from my experience, and let's see if you agree. In my pre-teen years, I went through a period of rebellion. I was still active in church with my family, so I went to youth camp in the summers. However, I was also active in the world, so I went to some crazy

---

[12] Psa. 9:11.
[13] Psa. 30:4.
[14] Psa. 30:12.
[15] Psa. 47:6-7.

rock concerts in the summers. My parents knew about the youth camps, but they weren't so aware of the rock concerts.

At the civic center in Monroe, Louisiana, I went to a 38 Special concert, and at another time, I even went to a Poison concert. I'm embarrassed to admit to that one, but I can say that I didn't even really know or like the band Poison. A few of my friends and I got free tickets to the concert, so we went. As I look back, it's interesting to me that there were some similarities in what happened in these rock concerts and youth events. There was hype and excitement about the event. There were dark rooms and bright, amazing stage lights. There were people standing and shouting. There were people waving their hands and moving to the beat of the music. There was an emotion that was stirred up inside the attendees by the lights, sound, crowds, and excitement. That year, I saw all of this happen at a 38 Special Concert, and I saw these very same things happening at big youth events. But on Sunday, I didn't see any of that in our church with a piano and organ, singing hymns in a brightly lit sanctuary. What was going on?

Remember, God created us to sing and to praise him. Singing is a common and consistent way that God's people respond to him. However, if we aren't responding to who God is and what he's done as the reason we sing, then we either don't sing, or we're waiting for the music and the environment to make us want to sing. If our thoughts of God don't make us want to sing, then something else will have to make us sing. If the heart for singing praise to God isn't already in our hearts, then we become worshipers of the band that stirs our emotions or to a style of music that makes us want to sing. If we are worshiping God in our hearts, however, we should sing to him. We should want to sing with no instruments or with lots of instruments. We should want to sing in the dark or in bright light. We should want to sing to a melody we know or to a melody we can learn. We should want to sing.

When we are worshiping God in our hearts, we come to worship -- any true worship service -- ready to sing and to lift our voices to praise our Lord. Is there emotion connected to our praise in song? At times, yes, but that emotion should be driven by the words of the songs as they proclaim the marvelous truth of God and express the deep, sometimes hard to express desires of our hearts towards our God. Emotions that are depending on the style of music or the excitement of the setting aren't emotions flowing out of worship. These are emotions that come from something else.

So do you sing to the Lord? Does the worship of God in your heart overflow into a joyful noise of worship in song? I want to challenge you to take a minute and use the ESV.org website to search for "sing praises," applying search options to restrict your search to the book of Psalms. Take time to read the verses displayed in your search results. What do these verses reveal about God's desire for you to sing praises to him? Maybe this is a good time to stop reading and start singing. Because of who God is and what God has done, sing to the Lord!

Sing New Songs

In examining the early, responsive songs of praise that God's people sang to him, it's important to note that these were new songs. They were necessarily new songs because they were immediately responding to what God had just done for his people. As God delivered his people from captivity in Egypt, God's people sang praise to him, proclaiming what he had done. As God delivered his people from King Jabin, God's people sang praise to him, proclaiming what he had done. These new songs were not only praise to God from the grateful hearts of his people, but these new songs were also declarations and proclamations of the mighty work of God for his people.

Scripture not only gives us the history of new songs that were sung in the past, but it also gives us prophecies about new songs that will be sung in the future. Through the glimpses into heaven that the Lord provides in the book of Revelation, we see new songs that are sung in heaven. As God's final plans for the redemption of creation and the judgment of sin unfold, there are new songs that are sung to the Lord by his people, who are responding to what he is doing by singing new songs of praise.

> And they sang a new song, saying, "Worthy are you to take the scroll and to open its seals, for you were slain, and by your blood you ransomed people for God from every tribe and language and people and nation."[16]

> . . . and they were singing a new song before the throne and before the four living creatures and before the elders. No one could learn that song except the 144,000 who had been redeemed from the earth.[17]

These pictures of the singing of new songs to the Lord give us a compelling reason to sing fresh, new songs to the Lord, who is still

---

[16] Rev. 5:9.
[17] Rev. 14:3.

actively at work delivering his people and fulfilling his promises. However, the most profound reason to sing new songs is that the Lord commanded us to sing new songs. In the book of Psalms, as well as the book of Isaiah, God directly commands his people to sing new songs to him.

> Sing to him a new song; play skillfully on the strings, with loud shouts.[18]

> Oh sing to the LORD a new song; sing to the LORD, all the earth![19]

> Oh sing to the LORD a new song, for he has done marvelous things! His right hand and his holy arm have worked salvation for him.[20]

> Praise the LORD! Sing to the LORD a new song, his praise in the assembly of the godly![21]

> Sing to the LORD a new song, his praise from the end of the earth, you who go down to the sea, and all that fills it, the coastlands and their inhabitants.[22]

Why does God command that new songs be sung? Perhaps it has something to do with the very nature of worship, which follows the biblical pattern of revelation and response. If God is actively at work in the lives of his people — and if God's people are actively

---

[18] Psa. 33:3.
[19] Psa. 96:1.
[20] Psa. 98:1.
[21] Psa. 149:1.
[22] Isa. 42:10.

experiencing the revelation of the Lord through his Word and through his work in their lives and in the world — then they will have much to praise the Lord about through new songs.

Honestly, I think this is one area of God's Word that is either unknown or ignored by many of God's people. To help us with perspective, a little history would be helpful. From the testimony of Scripture to worship flowing out of the Reformation, congregational singing played a part in worship, and just as with the examples in Scripture, great times of singing and songwriting have often followed great movements of God in history. In the Christian church, perhaps one of the most significant periods of congregational music occurred during and after the Reformation. It was in the Reformation — and particularly the third wave of the Reformation — that congregational singing began to grow in significance and in practice. This is when the writing of congregational hymns really began to develop.[23]

During this time in history, God was doing things in the lives of his people, reviving His Word and the gospel, and his people were responding with grateful hearts of worship by singing new songs to him. In modern times, during the 1960s and 1970s, the Lord was doing a work in the hearts of many young people around our country. The development and rise of praise songs started to emerge as God's people were expressing thanks in musical expressions that were familiar to them. Even today, we may hear a new song and immediately say, "That's it!" The song allowed the expression of your experience right now in your relationship with the Lord and in all that he was doing in your life.

---

[23] Davies, 69 and 93-96.

While there are great hymns from the Reformation, wonderful praise songs from decades ago, and even newer, sacred songs that connect with our hearts in worship, God doesn't want our singing to stop with the songs that have been written. God doesn't want us to stay stuck in the past, only using the songs of previous generations to praise him. He's working in our generation. He's working in our lives today. He wants us to sing new songs to him!

Sing Different Types of Songs

New songs, however, aren't the only kind of songs that we are commanded to sing to the Lord. It's interesting that in the New Testament there are only 14 verses that explicitly mention singing. Two of these verses are parallel verses, so that leaves only 12 unique verses referencing singing. In examining these unique verses, most are descriptive or illustrative. For example, a verse may be descriptive in simply mentioning that a hymn was sung,[24] or a verse may be illustrative, using singing as an illustration to help bring understanding to the truth that is being revealed in the verse or passage.[25] In looking at the remaining verses, there are only three verses in the New Testament that deal with singing in an instructive way. One of these verses is in the book of James, where those who are cheerful are instructed to sing.

> Is anyone among you suffering? Let him pray. Is anyone cheerful? Let him sing praise.[26]

---

[24] Matt. 26:40 and Acts 16:25.
[25] Matt. 11:17 and 1 Cor. 14:15.
[26] Jas. 5:13.

The final two verses that are instructive are very similar to one another. These verses are found in Ephesians and Colossians.

> . . . addressing one another in psalms and hymns and spiritual songs, singing and making melody to the Lord with your heart.[27]

> Let the word of Christ dwell in you richly, teaching and admonishing one another in all wisdom, singing psalms and hymns and spiritual songs, with thankfulness in your hearts to God.[28]

These two verses use the exact same terminology to define the types of songs that the church is to sing when they gather, which are defined as "psalms," "hymns," and "spiritual songs." From these verses, a couple of things are crystal clear for the church when it comes to worship in song. First, singing is meant for the edification or building up of the church. Believers are encouraged to address one another in singing. This doesn't mean that Christians are to be a living musical like Mary Poppins. It does mean this, however: When the church is gathered, individuals are singing not just between themselves and the Lord, but they are singing for one another as well. In the words of the songs and in the worship through the songs, there is an edifying and teaching aspect to singing when the church is gathered.

Second, the church is meant to sing a variety of songs. Why, though, would God want us to sing a variety of songs? Perhaps the reason is connected to the reality that singing is a communicative response of

---

[27] Eph. 5:19.
[28] Col. 3:16.

praise to God. We are to sing songs that are connected to the history of God's work for his people and that remind us how to praise God from the highs to the lows of life, such as is seen repeatedly in the book of Psalms. We are to sing Psalms. We are to sing songs that are grounded in the Word of God and filled with the truth of God, teaching and admonishing us in the right theology of God. We are to sing hymns. Finally, we are to sing songs that are expressive of the reality of our relationship with God and his active work in our lives and in the world. We are to sing spiritual songs. While the style of music (instrumentation, etc.) can remain the same or change from one song to another, we should use different types of songs to express the range of purpose in God's design for worshiping him through song.

When we were raising our children, they were so different in so many ways. They were different in age and gender. They had different personalities and interests. They liked different foods and T.V. shows. So, my wife and I decided to try to cater to their individual preferences. Since Tiffany liked to cook for our family, she would cook two meals every night to make sure Alaina and Cade only had to eat what they liked and never had to put up with eating something that they didn't like. She even would cook on the schedule that met their preference for when they wanted to eat. One meal would be prepared a little earlier, since one of them liked to eat early, and the other meal would be prepared a little later, since the other liked to eat late at night. We also built a room divider, which divided our family room into two parts. We set up two televisions with headphones so that the children only had to watch the T.V. shows they liked and didn't have to share or wait for the other person.

Hopefully, most of you reading this are thinking, "He's got to be kidding. This is ridiculous!" If so, you're right. There's no way that we did all of that. Tiffany only cooked one meal, and our children learned to eat it and like it -- or at least not say anything bad about the food. They had to share the T.V. and learn to sacrifice and wait, letting one person get to watch something they liked while waiting their turn to watch what they wanted to watch. Why did we do this with our children? We chose not to cater to our children's preferences because it was good for them. We're a family, and part of being a family is learning to give and to sacrifice. We're a family, and learning to do things together rather than separately is a part of being a family.

We don't want to make a ridiculous mistake when it comes to worship in song in our churches. We're a family, and we must act like a family. Catering to groups within the church based on musical preferences encourages division rather than unity in the church. Catering to groups within the church based on musical preferences encourages selfish worship and a lack of sacrifice and submission to one another out of reverence for Christ. Catering to groups within the church based on musical preferences results in people leaving the church because of the style of songs being sung -- or not sung -- with no regard to the theological content of the songs that are sung. All of this is ridiculous, and none of this is biblical.

Singing is one important overflow of the Spirit and the Word of Christ dwelling in us as believers. When we sing together, we do it for the purpose of praising our God and for building one another up. This is God's wisdom in commanding us to sing new songs and to sing different types of songs. A variety of types of songs is good for our spiritual diet. It teaches us sacrifice and love for one another.

It's obedient to the Word of God, so sing! Sing new songs to the Lord, and sing a variety of songs when you gather to worship to glorify the Lord and to edify his church.

Take time to work through the questions below as you consider singing in personal and corporate worship. Worship in song is such an important aspect of corporate worship. It's true that it is often divisive because it's often driven by personal preference rather than theology. It's also true that music is communication and that we all connect more readily with certain types of music that allow us to more naturally communicate. It's also true that God's desire is that music in worship is for edifying and building up the church more than it's for personal gratification. These are tough truths for our hearts to wrestle with and for us to submit to in our lives, so take the time to work out what God's Word is doing in your heart when it comes to worship through song in your life.

Applying God's Truth

> (1) Look through the song of Moses in Exodus 15. How was this song responsive to what the Lord had just done for his people? How did singing allow all of God's people to express their praise to him together at that time? Today, are our songs responsive to what the Lord has done? How does singing when we gather as the church allow all of us to express our praise to the Lord together?

> (2) Do you sing praises to the Lord? Is singing – whether in-tune or out-of-tune – a part of your regular worship of God?

(3) How do new songs testify to the fresh experience or reality of God's relationship with his people and our relationship with him?

(4) Why does God command us to sing new songs? What is significant about this in connection to our response to his revelation? Why are new songs important for worship?

(5) Why are some of us so resistant to new songs and new music in worship? How can we become more faithful to God's desire for the expression of our praise through new songs?

(6) How do we use Psalms in our praise in song today? Why are Psalms important to use?

(7) Hymns are known for their scriptural truth. Why would God desire that we sing hymns to him in gathered worship?

(8) Spiritual songs are those songs of praise and testimony that fall outside of Psalms and hymns. Why would God desire that we sing spiritual songs to him?

(9) What does this chapter say about division in the church over preferences in music in the church? Pray for unity in your church and for worship in song in your church to be driven by theology and not by personal preference.

Chapter 5:
The Word

Throughout Scripture, one thing that was consistent in the lives of God's people was his Word. Through the spoken word, God created all things in heaven and on earth. Through the spoken word, God pursued Adam and Eve when they were hiding from him after they had sinned. Through the spoken word, God made a promise to Abraham and his descendants. Through the spoken word, God gave Israel the Law. Through the spoken word, God called his people to covenant faithfulness through the prophets. Through Jesus, the Word became flesh and dwelt among us, and through the spoken word, Jesus clarified the law and proclaimed the Kingdom of God. Through the spoken word, Jesus called sinners to repent and believe. Through the spoken word, Jesus gave the church its mission until his return. Through the spoken word, Peter proclaimed the gospel and thousands came to repentance and faith in Jesus Christ at Pentecost!

We could go on and on, but the point is clear: God's Word has always been essential to God's work in the world in the lives of his people. God hasn't changed, and his Word is still essential to his work today. Therefore, God's Word is also integral to worship today. How do we know this is true? Because his Word clearly shows us through example and command that proclaiming and responding to the Word of God is an important expression in our worship of God. The pattern of worship through revelation and response is reinforced and encouraged through the preaching and teaching of God's Word. In fact, we see that the revelatory nature of God's

Word demands a response from those who hear his Word. His Word is foundational to worship.

Proclaiming God's Word

In the Old Testament, great moments of revival among God's people were often connected to beautiful moments of proclaiming and teaching the Word of God to God's people. There's no better example of this than in Nehemiah 8, where Ezra gathered the leaders and God's people, and God's Word became the center of their attention. For hours, God's Word was read and explained to his people. It was a worship service that was word-saturated, and it was needed. God's people needed to know their God, and they needed to know what their God required of them. The Word was -- and still is -- the best way that people can know their God and know what God requires of them. Consider this scene from Nehemiah 8 as it points to the priority of the Word and the hunger in the hearts of God's people for his Word.

> And all the people gathered as one man into the square before the Water Gate. And they told Ezra the scribe to bring the Book of the Law of Moses that the LORD had commanded Israel. So Ezra the priest brought the Law before the assembly, both men and women and all who could understand what they heard, on the first day of the seventh month. And he read from it facing the square before the Water Gate from early morning until midday, in the presence of the men and the women and those who could understand. And the ears of all the people were attentive to the Book of the

> Law. And Ezra the scribe stood on a wooden platform that they had made for the purpose . . .[1]

> They read from the book, from the Law of God, clearly, and they gave the sense, so that the people understood the reading.[2]

At the time of Ezra and Nehemiah, during the return of the Jews from exile, the structure of synagogue worship was developing. While the temple served as the place for sacrifices and national gatherings, the temple had been destroyed. The people of God had been deported from Jerusalem. So the synagogue developed and served as the place of local, daily, and weekly gathering for worship. Sacrifices weren't offered in the synagogue, though. The synagogue was the local place of worship that consisted of prayer, praise, and the Word.

By the time of Jesus, synagogues were common, and in synagogue worship, there was a significant focus on reading and discussing God's Word. There were selections "from the Law and the Prophets" for synagogue worship each day, and some of the male congregants who attended the synagogue services would often participate in the reading of the Scriptures.[3] The lesson from a reading would then follow, and if there was someone present who could preach, the ruler of the synagogue may ask him to speak.[4] As we'll explore below, Jesus validated worship in the synagogues through his own participation in synagogue worship. Additionally, worship through the Word in synagogues became a popular avenue

---

[1] Neh. 8:1-4.
[2] Neh. 8:8.
[3] Davies, 18.
[4] Ibid.

for the preaching and teaching ministry of Jesus, as well as his disciples who would continue his pattern of attending services and preaching the gospel in the synagogues.[5]

In his hometown, Jesus was invited in the synagogue to read one of the Scripture passages for that day, and as tradition allowed, Jesus then followed the reading of the Scripture by commenting on God's Word. He explained and applied the passage to his hearers.

> And Jesus returned in the power of the Spirit to Galilee, and a report about him went out through all the surrounding country. And he taught in their synagogues, being glorified by all. And he came to Nazareth, where he had been brought up. And as was his custom, he went to the synagogue on the Sabbath day, and he stood up to read. And the scroll of the prophet Isaiah was given to him. He unrolled the scroll and found the place where it was written, "The Spirit of the Lord is upon me, because he has anointed me to proclaim good news to the poor. He has sent me to proclaim liberty to the captives and recovering of sight to the blind, to set at liberty those who are oppressed, to proclaim the year of the Lord's favor." And he rolled up the scroll and gave it back to the attendant and sat down. And the eyes of all in the synagogue were fixed on him. And he began to say to them, "Today this Scripture has been fulfilled in your hearing."[6]

---

[5] Acts 13:13-16; 14:1; 17:1, 10, and 17; 18:1-4, 24-26; 19:8; 22:19.
[6] Luke 4:14-21.

In the book of Acts, as the first church was started, the preaching and teaching of the Word was seen as central to the church as they gathered weekly and daily in homes to worship. They devoted themselves to the apostle's teaching, which was likely the oral stories and teachings of Jesus, which were eventually written down as the Gospels that we have today. Surely, the apostle's teaching also included the application of the gospel into the lives of believers and into the life of the church, which is the function of God's Word that is captured in most of the letters in the New Testament. Consider the consistency and devotion to the Word in the worship of the early church.

> And they devoted themselves to the apostles' teaching and the fellowship, to the breaking of bread and the prayers.[7]

> And every day, in the temple and from house to house, they did not cease teaching and preaching that the Christ is Jesus.[8]

What was consistent in the examples of Nehemiah, Jesus, and the early church? Reading, explaining, and applying God's Word was an important expression of worship when God's people gathered for worship. That was true then, and it still is true today. Throughout the history of Christian worship, the Word has always been a part of gathered worship.[9] It's important to realize, though, that God's Word is not only an important part of worship through the example of God's people, but his Word is also an important part of worship

---

[7] Acts 2:42.
[8] Acts 5:42.
[9] Bryan Chapell, *Christ-Centered Worship: Letting the Gospel Shape our Practice* (Grand Rapids: Baker Academic, 2016), 222-223.

based on his instruction and command. For the New Testament church, God's instruction for the use of his Word in worship is perhaps seen most clearly through the words of the apostle Paul to the young elder, Timothy. Paul said this to him:

> Until I come, devote yourself to the public reading of Scripture, to exhortation, to teaching. Do not neglect the gift you have, which was given you by prophecy when the council of elders laid their hands on you. Practice these things, immerse yourself in them, so that all may see your progress. Keep a close watch on yourself and on the teaching. Persist in this, for by so doing you will save both yourself and your hearers.[10]

The proclamation of God's Word is essential to the ongoing sanctification of God's people. It's foundational to the pattern of revelation and response in worship, and it's also necessary for the evangelization of the lost. God's Word is what the Lord uses to grow faith in the hearts of his people. The Lord presented the logic of this through the apostle Paul in the following, powerful questions and answers in Romans 10.

> How then will they call on him in whom they have not believed? And how are they to believe in him of whom they have never heard? And how are they to hear without someone preaching? And how are they to preach unless they are sent? As it is written, "How beautiful are the feet of those who preach the good news!" But they have not all obeyed the

---

[10] 1 Tim. 4:13-16.

gospel. For Isaiah says, "Lord, who has believed what he has heard from us?" So faith comes from hearing, and hearing through the word of Christ.[11]

These words come to life in the Acts of the Apostles, where the focus on the "word" is seen as critical to the work of the gospel and the advance of the church.

> And the word of God continued to increase, and the number of the disciples multiplied greatly in Jerusalem, and a great many of the priests became obedient to the faith.[12]
>
> But the word of God increased and multiplied.[13]
>
> And the word of the Lord was spreading throughout the whole region.[14]
>
> So the word of the Lord continued to increase and prevail mightily.[15]

These verses are only a few of the many verses that emphasize the work of the "word" in the early church in the book of Acts. I would encourage you to take time to go to ESV.org and do a word search for "word," filtering your results to the book of Acts in the New Testament. Read through these verses, and you'll see the constant emphasis in the ministry of the Word in the work of the gospel and

---

[11] Rom. 10:14-17.
[12] Acts 6:7.
[13] Acts 12:24.
[14] Acts 13:49.
[15] Acts 19:20.

in the gathering of Jews in the synagogue and first-century believers in the church.

Today, the proclamation of the Word is still foundational to worship. This is especially true for many denominations coming out of the Reformation. In the Roman Catholic tradition, the communion table is central, and the priest stands in front of it, acting as the mediator between the Lord's Supper and the Lord's people. The pulpit takes a place of lesser prominence, communicating visually that the Eucharist is central to Catholic worship. However, in the traditions flowing out of the Reformation, this changed. The pulpit took center stage, often elevated above the communion table, and the communion table was placed in front of the minister, eliminating the pastor as the mediator between the Lord's people and his supper. All of this was to communicate something important about worship, and the centrality of the pulpit communicated that God's Word was central when God's people gathered to worship.[16]

Responding to God's Word

If we re-examine the pictures of God's Word in worship in the lives of post-exilic Jews, in the life of Jesus in the synagogue, and in the life of the early church, it's interesting to see that there are only two, basic ways to respond to the Word of God.

One response is seen in Nehemiah and Acts. In both of these accounts, worship through the Word is emphasized in the gathering of God's people, and in both accounts, as God's Word is rightly read, explained, and applied, God's people respond in worship. They heard the Word of God. They understood the Word of God, and

---

[16] Webber, 151-160.

they believed and were obedient to God's Word. In the case of Nehemiah, God's people understood how far they were from God's design for his covenant nation, and they mourned and repented in response to this realization. Nehemiah and Ezra told them not to mourn but rather to rejoice for the wonderful grace of God that came to them through the Word.[17] In the book of Acts, as God's people heard the Word of God taught and preached, they responded in grateful obedience to the Word of God, which was seen in their generosity, unity, worship, ministry, and multiplication.[18] In both cases, God revealed to us the essence of worship through the Word, which is faith and obedience to the Word in the life of the worshiper. However, there is another response to God's Word even when it's rightly read, explained, and applied, and that response is rejection.

In the synagogue in his hometown, Jesus correctly read, explained, and applied God's Word, but the hearers would not accept the truth of God's Word. They rejected Jesus and his message, and in fact, they desired to murder him for the truth that he proclaimed. When confronted with their sinful, hardened hearts, they rejected God's Word rather than rejecting their sin.[19] In this case, worship through the Word didn't happen. Here's what I think is important for us to recognize: What these examples emphasize is that worship through the Word occurs when hearts believe and obediently respond to God's Word in worship. This is much easier said than done.

Years ago, I worked on a cattle farm in north Louisiana. The farm had sent me to Kansas to learn how to pregnancy check cows. I enjoyed the learning process, and through the school, I became

---

[17] Neh. 8:9-12.
[18] Acts 2:43-47.
[19] Lk. 4:14-44.

pretty good at "preg checking," which was a useful skill on the farm. One of my co-workers, however, was more skeptical than accepting of my new skill, and it didn't take long before he disagreed with my assessment of a particular cow. This cow was not only pregnant, but she was about to give birth! My co-worker outranked me, though, and he refused to believe that she was pregnant. I even tried to get him to check the cow himself, encouraging him to let me show him what to look for so that he could feel the calf for himself, but he ignored me. Against my strong protest, we put the cow with the group of cows that weren't pregnant, and we sent her off to pasture that was not suitable for calving cows.

Within days, the cow gave birth to a healthy calf, but because she was in a rough area of the farm with a rugged creek bottom flowing through the pasture, she gave birth in the creek bottom. It was winter, and the calf didn't have the strength to climb the sides of the creek to get to safety. By the time we found the calf, it was wet, half-frozen, and exhausted. Thankfully, we were able to get the calf and its mother to safety. We came very close to losing the calf that day. Why? The truth didn't line up with what someone thought he saw and understood, so he rejected the truth.

When God's Word is proclaimed, there's always a response. The response can be negative, ranging from indifference to rejection, and this shouldn't alarm us. The Lord's truth is counter to the world's truth. God's ways are not our ways. It's only through the illuminating work of the Holy Spirit that someone can understand God's Word and be led to a conviction that leads to repentance. However, when the Lord is at work in someone's life, the response can be positive, moving the hearer to believe and to obey. This is worship through the Word! When God's Word is proclaimed and his people respond in faith and obedience, worship is happening. God is revealing himself and his truth, and his people are responding to that revelation in faith and obedience. This leads us to the final reality about the Word as an element in our worship.

God's Word is Essential

In south Louisiana, we often deal with hurricanes. These weather events can range from a little bit of wind and rain to absolute devastation, and with almost every hurricane, there's uncertainty on where the storm will hit and just how bad the storm will be in any specific location until the last day and hours before landfall. Because of the uncertainty and rapidly changing conditions, preparation is important. I was reminded of this during the 2020 hurricane season in the area where we live in south Louisiana.

I wasn't as prepared as I should have been. I had the generator ready to go, but I didn't have the equipment at our house to deal with the aftermath of the storm. I wasn't expecting the storm to be as bad as it ended up being; therefore, I wasn't expecting the tree-sized limbs and sections of trees that fell in our yard. I was reminded that one of the most essential things for after the storm was good neighbors! Neighbors with chainsaws, 4-wheelers, tractors, and trailers were an incredible blessing. Without these essential things, the big, tree-sized limbs would have laid in our driveway, road, and yard for days. This experience reminded me yet again of why it's essential to have the essentials that are needed when a hurricane is approaching. In fact, this preparation principle can apply to many things that are important in our lives, and it certainly applies to the most important things in life, such as worship.

When it comes to worship, God's Word provides ample evidence that the Word of God is essential when God's people are gathered for worship. The essential nature of the Word is seen in many ways in Scripture, so let's explore just a few examples of the ways that God's Word is seen as essential in worship.

First, God's Word is essential for salvation. By God's design, faith that leads to repentance and salvation comes through hearing the Word of God. Jesus himself emphasized this by stating clearly that rejection of the Word is rejection of the God of the Word. Salvation — eternal life — will only come to those who accept Christ and his Word. These truths aren't isolated statements in a single verse, but they are repeated truths that are consistent throughout God's Word. Take these few examples from the Gospel of John and the letter to the Romans, and spend some time researching and finding other passages that reinforce these same truths.

> ". . . Truly, truly, I say to you, if anyone keeps my word, he will never see death."[20]

> "I do not ask for these only, but also for those who will believe in me through their word . . ."[21]

> So faith comes from hearing, and hearing through the word of Christ.[22]

Second, God's Word is essential for growth in Christ. Sanctification — growth in holiness in Christ — comes through the work of God through his Word in the life of the worshiper. The Word of God is

---

[20] John 8:51.
[21] John 17:20.
[22] Rom. 10:17.

sufficient for this work and is necessary for this work. God's chosen instrument for revealing himself to the world and for transforming the hearts and renewing the minds of his people is his Word. Explore these verses from the Gospel of John and a couple of the Letters in the New Testament that provide a basis for this truth.

> "Already you are clean because of the word that I have spoken to you."[23]

> All Scripture is breathed out by God and profitable for teaching, for reproof, for correction, and for training in righteousness.[24]

> For the word of God is living and active, sharper than any two-edged sword, piercing to the division of soul and of spirit, of joints and of marrow, and discerning the thoughts and intentions of the heart.[25]

Third, God's Word is essential for the work of God's leaders in the church. The main, differentiating requirement between the elder and the deacon in the church is the ability to teach. Why? Because the work of the Word — teaching and preaching God's Word — is essential to the task of God's leaders in the church, which points to the essential nature of the Word in gathered worship that God's leaders are called to lead. Read through these sample verses from the Pastoral Letters in the New Testament, and then see if you can find

---

[23] John 15:3.
[24] 2 Tim. 3:16.
[25] Heb. 4:12.

others that consistently state the importance of the ministry of the Word in the work of church leaders.

> Therefore an overseer must be above reproach, the husband of one wife, sober-minded, self-controlled, respectable, hospitable, able to teach. [26]

> Until I come, devote yourself to the public reading of Scripture, to exhortation, to teaching.[27]

> . . . and what you have heard from me in the presence of many witnesses entrust to faithful men, who will be able to teach others also.[28]

> . . . preach the word; be ready in season and out of season; reprove, rebuke, and exhort, with complete patience and teaching.[29]

> He must hold firm to the trustworthy word as taught, so that he may be able to give instruction in sound doctrine and also to rebuke those who contradict it.[30]

Finally, God's Word is essential for obedience to the Great Commission of Christ. The church is called to make disciples, and a necessary function of disciple making is teaching them to observe all that Christ commanded.

---

[26] 1 Tim. 3:2.
[27] 1 Tim. 4:13.
[28] 2 Tim. 2:2.
[29] 2 Tim. 4:2.
[30] Titus 1:9.

> And Jesus came and said to them, "All authority in heaven and on earth has been given to me. Go therefore and make disciples of all nations, baptizing them in the name of the Father and of the Son and of the Holy Spirit, teaching them to observe all that I have commanded you. And behold, I am with you always, to the end of the age."[31]

To carry this commandment out, the church must teach and preach the Word of God. The Word is essential to the mission, purpose, and work of the church. So if we put all of this evidence together, it's clear that God's Word is essential in gathered worship in order to accomplish God's work and his purpose through his people. God's Word is essential for making disciples. It's essential for growing disciples of Jesus Christ, and it's essential to fulfilling the work of the church that God's leaders are called to do.

In our church, we prioritize the preaching of God's Word in our worship because it is essential to our worship. It is the most important revelation of God to us. It is the way that God continues to speak to us. God's Word contains the words of life that are essential for bringing life to God's people. God's Word is necessary for making disciples, which includes leading people to salvation through repentance and faith in Jesus and growing people in the holiness of Jesus Christ our Lord. God's Word brings the revelation of God to us that provides the opportunity for response from us. It fuels our worship both personally and corporately.

---

[31] Matt. 28:18-20.

Take time to work through the questions below, applying this chapter to worship through the Word in your life and in your church.

Applying God's Truth

(1) How do we emphasize God's Word in our worship gatherings each week? Is the Word read, explained, and applied? Using the passages above (or other passages), why is this important in our gathered worship?

(2) Read Acts 2:43-47. How do you see the evidence of the words of Christ in the lives of Christ's followers? How do we see that in our church today?

(3) How did the people in the synagogue in Luke 4 react to God's Word that Jesus read, explained, and applied? Do people still react like that today? Have you ever reacted like that to God's convicting truth? Why?

(4) How has this chapter changed, reinforced, or encouraged your view of worship through the Word of God?

Chapter 6:
The Lord's Supper

In the New Testament, the uniquely Old Testament sacrificial system ended through the final sacrifice of Jesus. The Lord's Supper became a uniquely New Testament expression of worship, remembering the death of Jesus for our sin and celebrating the presence of God with us. It became an ongoing reminder of the final and complete sacrifice for sin.

A Lamb Sacrificed

When the final plague was about to be poured out on Egypt, God's mercy was displayed in the midst of his judgement against the Egyptians. He provided a way for the plague to pass over the Israelites. In Exodus 12, God commanded the Israelites to take lambs and to sacrifice the lambs on a certain day, wiping the blood of the sacrificed lambs on the doorposts of their homes. The homes that were covered in the substitutionary blood of the lamb were passed over during the plague.

> The LORD said to Moses and Aaron in the land of Egypt, "This month shall be for you the beginning of months. It shall be the first month of the year for you. Tell all the congregation of Israel that on the tenth day of this month every man shall take a lamb according to their fathers' houses, a lamb for a household. And if the household is too small for a lamb, then he and his nearest neighbor shall take according to the number of persons; according to what each can eat you shall make your count for the

lamb. Your lamb shall be without blemish, a male a year old. You may take it from the sheep or from the goats, and you shall keep it until the fourteenth day of this month, when the whole assembly of the congregation of Israel shall kill their lambs at twilight. "Then they shall take some of the blood and put it on the two doorposts and the lintel of the houses in which they eat it. They shall eat the flesh that night, roasted on the fire; with unleavened bread and bitter herbs they shall eat it. Do not eat any of it raw or boiled in water, but roasted, its head with its legs and its inner parts. And you shall let none of it remain until the morning; anything that remains until the morning you shall burn. In this manner you shall eat it: with your belt fastened, your sandals on your feet, and your staff in your hand. And you shall eat it in haste. It is the LORD's Passover. For I will pass through the land of Egypt that night, and I will strike all the firstborn in the land of Egypt, both man and beast; and on all the gods of Egypt I will execute judgments: I am the LORD. The blood shall be a sign for you, on the houses where you are. And when I see the blood, I will pass over you, and no plague will befall you to destroy you, when I strike the land of Egypt.[32]

---

[32] Exod. 12:1-13.

Later in history, when the time had come for Jesus to enter his public ministry, John the Baptist declared that Jesus was "the Lamb of God, who takes away the sin of the world!"[33] Then Jesus, in his last meal with his disciples, gave new meaning to the Passover meal, associating the bread with his body that was given for them and the wine with his blood that was "poured out for many for the forgiveness of sins."[34]

> Now on the first day of Unleavened Bread the disciples came to Jesus, saying, "Where will you have us prepare for you to eat the Passover?" He said, "Go into the city to a certain man and say to him, 'The Teacher says, My time is at hand. I will keep the Passover at your house with my disciples.'" And the disciples did as Jesus had directed them, and they prepared the Passover.[35]

> Now as they were eating, Jesus took bread, and after blessing it broke it and gave it to the disciples, and said, "Take, eat; this is my body." And he took a cup, and when he had given thanks he gave it to them, saying, "Drink of it, all of you, for this is my blood of the covenant, which is poured out for many for the forgiveness of sins. I tell you I will not drink again of this fruit of the vine until that day when I drink it new with you in my Father's kingdom."[36]

---

[33] John 1:29.
[34] Matt. 26:28.
[35] Matt. 26:17-19.
[36] Matt. 26:26-29.

The early church understood what had happened after the death of Jesus. They understood what Jesus had done: That Jesus was the Passover lamb who was sacrificed for the sins of God's people. Paul made this clear in his letter to the church in Corinth.

> Cleanse out the old leaven that you may be a new lump, as you really are unleavened. For Christ, our Passover lamb, has been sacrificed.[37]

The Passover was a symbolic meal, representing God's redemption of Israel. It reminded God's people of his mercy towards them and laid the understanding of the sacrificial lamb that would bring deliverance to God's people. However, while the Passover was a reminder of God's deliverance of his people from Egypt, the Passover was not a reminder of a full and final deliverance from their sin. The Passover pointed towards a better sacrifice and a complete sacrifice, which was the sacrifice of Jesus, the Lamb of God, who died for the forgiveness of sin. The Lord's Supper reminds us of the substitutionary death of Jesus for sin, which brings God's eternal deliverance to his people. The Lord's Supper replaced the Passover for God's people. It is the meal that reveals and celebrates the final and completed work of the true sacrificial Lamb of God, Jesus Christ our Lord.

A Meal to Remember

When God gave the Passover meal to the people of Israel, his instructions made it clear that this meal was intended to be something that Israel would continue to practice year-to-year. The meal was designed to be a memorial to this moment in the lives of

---

[37] 1 Cor. 5:7.

God's people. He wanted them to never forget — to always remember — the deliverance that he provided them through the final plague. Additionally, God commanded them to explain this to the generations to come. He wanted his people to continue to proclaim the meaning of the Passover meal so that future generations would understand how the Passover represented God's gracious deliverance of his people through the blood of the sacrificed lamb.

> "This day shall be for you a memorial day, and you shall keep it as a feast to the LORD; throughout your generations, as a statute forever, you shall keep it as a feast.[38]
>
> And when you come to the land that the LORD will give you, as he has promised, you shall keep this service. And when your children say to you, 'What do you mean by this service?' you shall say, 'It is the sacrifice of the LORD's Passover, for he passed over the houses of the people of Israel in Egypt, when he struck the Egyptians but spared our houses.'" And the people bowed their heads and worshiped.[39]

As the early church practiced the Lord's supper week-to-week, they understood the same design for the Lord's Supper as the Lord's design for the Passover meal, which was remembrance and proclamation. In Paul's instructions on the Lord's Supper, he reminded the church that the Lord's Supper was to be taken in

---

[38] Exod. 12:14.
[39] Exod. 12:25-27.

remembrance of the substitutionary sacrifice of Jesus on the cross, remembering his blood that was shed for the forgiveness of sin. The Lord's Supper is a memorial of the Lord's sacrifice that brings deliverance to his people through the blood of the sacrificial Lamb. Additionally, the Lord's Supper is a proclamation of the Lord's death until Christ returns.

> For I received from the Lord what I also delivered to you, that the Lord Jesus on the night when he was betrayed took bread, and when he had given thanks, he broke it, and said, "This is my body, which is for you. Do this in remembrance of me." In the same way also he took the cup, after supper, saying, "This cup is the new covenant in my blood. Do this, as often as you drink it, in remembrance of me." For as often as you eat this bread and drink the cup, you proclaim the Lord's death until he comes.[40]

In this way, the Lord gave the church a beautiful way to remember the gospel and to proclaim the gospel as they came together to worship each week.

At one time, the local elementary school in our area had a program called the "Reader Leader Program." It was a wonderful program that allowed our community to engage with our school, connecting volunteers with first graders in our school system in order to help encourage reading. Volunteers would be assigned a child for the school year, and the volunteer could go to the school once or more a week to read books in the school library with their child. When I

---

[40] 1 Cor. 11:23-26.

would go at the start of the school day, we'd always have to stand to salute and to say the pledge of allegiance to the U.S. flag. The children would also recite their school motto and other things that were deemed important to know. Why? Because we want them to know and to remember things that were important: Our nation's pledge, their school motto, good life habits, etc. Repetition is an important part of learning and remembering, and this is by God's design in how he created us. It's why he gave the Passover to Israel in the Old Testament and the Lord's Supper to his church now. What's important is that the church should celebrate the Lord's Supper regularly — and often if following the practice of the early church — because it is an important way that we proclaim God's redemption through Christ.

At the death of Jesus on the cross, he cried out "it is finished,"[41] and the curtain in the temple was torn.[42] This curtain separated God's presence from his people. The curtain was there to protect sinful people from the holy, consuming presence of God. But when the Lamb of God was sacrificed for the forgiveness of sin, the curtain was torn. God's presence with his people was possible. The work and purpose of the temple and the sacrificial system was complete. Through faith, God's people were "sanctified through the offering of the body of Jesus Christ once for all."[43]

> And every priest stands daily at his service, offering repeatedly the same sacrifices, which can never take away sins. But when Christ had offered for all time

---

[41] John 19:30.
[42] Matt. 27:51.
[43] Heb. 10:10.

> a single sacrifice for sins, he sat down at the right hand of God[44]

> For by a single offering he has perfected for all time those who are being sanctified.[45]

For the early Jewish Christians, it was like worship at the temple and the synagogue had been merged together as they gathered for prayer, praise, and the Word, and they remembered the all-sufficient sacrifice of Jesus Christ the Lamb of God. This was something to really celebrate!

The Lord's Supper is a reminder of the amazing grace of God. It reminds us that there is no need for the sacrificial system and for the temple to hide the presence of God from sinful people. God's presence is now with his people because the sacrifice for sin is finished. The sacrifice of Jesus was final and complete, and in this way, the Lord's Supper in Christian worship is a beautiful proclamation of the gospel. The Lord's Supper is a continuing celebration of God's gift of forgiveness through the completed work of Christ on the cross.

You know, there are some things that continue that become burdensome. We all have to eat, which usually means that we need to cook. I love to eat, and Tiffany enjoys cooking. These two things are good, but these two things mean that there's something else that must continue to happen: The dishes have to be cleaned. Washing dishes can become burdensome. Sometimes we may eat out or adjust what we're fixing just based on not wanting to do the dishes! Other

---

[44] Heb. 10:11-12.
[45] Heb. 10:14.

things, like the dishes, can become burdensome for us, such as mowing the grass, maintaining old vehicles, and medicating our aging bodies for all the growing aches and pains.

Although we learn to accept and to do these things, we can get tired of the constant demand of doing repetitive things. The sacrificial system had to have been that way for Israel. It must have been burdensome to always know that the sacrifice wasn't enough to fully forgive and that there was always going to be a next time and another sacrifice that would be required. The Lord's Supper proclaims that in Christ the sacrifice has been satisfied. There's no next time or another sacrifice that's needed. The Lord's Supper is both a solemn reminder of the death of Christ on the cross and a joyful celebration of the accomplished work of Christ on the cross.

A Meal to Share

The testimony of the early church in Acts makes it clear that the Lord's Supper was a common expression of worship as the church gathered together in homes in Jerusalem and in subsequent years throughout the Roman Empire. While "breaking bread" could refer to a meal that is shared, I believe the phrase in Acts 2 and 20 refers to the practice of the Lord's Supper.

> And they devoted themselves to the apostles' teaching and the fellowship, to the breaking of bread and the prayers.[46]
>
> On the first day of the week, when we were gathered together to break bread, Paul talked with

---

[46] Acts 2:42.

them, intending to depart on the next day, and he
prolonged his speech until midnight.[47]

As the church gathered regularly for worship, they regularly shared in the Lord's Supper, which often was connected to a meal that they shared as well. We see that this pattern continued in the churches that were planted around the Roman Empire as the gospel spread from Jerusalem to Judea, from Judea to Samaria, and from Samaria to the ends of the earth. We're given a glimpse into the reality of this as Paul gathered with the church in Troas and celebrated the Lord's Supper on the night before he planned to depart. Additionally, when the apostle Paul gave corrective instruction on the practice of the Lord's Supper to the church in Corinth, he repeatedly emphasized the fact that the Lord's Supper was something that the church did when the church came together.[48]

> So then, my brothers, when you come together to eat, wait for one another — if anyone is hungry, let him eat at home — so that when you come together it will not be for judgment . . . .[49]

In addition to the Scriptural evidence for the practice of the Lord's Supper, the historical witness of the church confirms this expression of worship when the church gathers. The Lord's Supper was practiced weekly in the gathering of the church until the Reformation period, at which point the imbalance of focus and the error in doctrine on the Lord's Supper in the Roman church was addressed by the reformers, leading to a reclaiming of the biblical doctrine of

---

[47] Acts 20:7.
[48] 1 Cor. 11:18, 20, and 33.
[49] 1 Cor. 11:33-34.

the Lord's Supper and to a less frequent practice of the Lord's Supper in some traditions coming out of the Reformation. However, the church continued to practice the Lord's Supper when it came together.

Think with me for a minute about a meal that most of us in the U.S. are very familiar with: Thanksgiving Dinner. For many of us, we gather with family on Thanksgiving, and if you're like our family, each family that participates in the Thanksgiving meal helps by cooking and bringing part of the meal to the gathering. The year 2020 was unusual for many of us on Thanksgiving. With concerns for older family members, many families decided not to get together in a large group. That was strange enough, but what if each family only cooked the part of the meal that they usually would cook and bring to the gathering. In other words, you cooked and ate the part of the meal that you usually prepared, and everyone else cooked and ate the part of the meal that they usually prepared. You never come together for the meal. In fact, it would never really be a meal at all, would it? None of us would try to do this on Thanksgiving. Why? It won't make sense. The point of the holiday and the meal is to be together. The point is to come together to celebrate and to be thankful. It wouldn't be a Thanksgiving meal if you weren't there, sharing with each other and spending time together.

The Lord's Supper is similar. It's a meal that's meant to be celebrated together. Sometimes, in areas where it's restricted and dangerous, such as in some communist or Islamic states, it may have to be done with only a few people and in places where believers can gather without suspicion. However, what's most important is that the Lord's Supper continues to be affirmed and to be practiced in Christian worship when the church comes together.

What does the Lord's Supper look like in your church? Is it practiced regularly? Is it shared with God's intent for the remembering and strengthening of the church? Use the following questions to assess your heart of worship through the Lord's Supper and the practice of the Lord's Supper in worship within your church.

Applying God's Truth

> (1) In Matthew 26, how does Jesus define what the bread represents? How does Jesus define what the wine represents? What does Jesus mean that his blood is poured out for many for the forgiveness of sin? How does this help interpret John's statements about the sins of the world?

> (2) When you celebrate the Lord's Supper with your church, do you accomplish the two purposes of remembrance and proclamation? Is so, how? If not, why?

> (3) Read Hebrews 10:1-18. How does this passage bring significance to the Lord's Supper as the Lord's Supper remembers and proclaims the death of Jesus?

(4) How often do you think we should observe the Lord's Supper when we gather as the church? Why? Make sure you base your final opinion on Scripture rather than tradition, since God's Word is our final and sufficient guide for our faith and the practice of our faith.

Conclusion

My prayer for this book was that God's Word would help bring biblical worship into focus in our heads and in our hearts. My hope was that this book would reinforce truths about worship that we know; remind us of truths that we may have forgotten; and reveal to us truths that we need to embrace. Worship should be what brings God's people together and brings great glory to our God. It's far too important to be driven by preferences rather than theology. It's far too important to be rooted in tradition in our lives and our churches rather than God's Word for our lives and his church. So my concluding question is this: Has this exploration of worship in God's Word helped bring biblical worship into focus in your head and in your heart?

To answer this question, I hope that you'll use this conclusion as a workbook to prayerfully assess what God's revealed from his Word to you and what his Word is calling you to do in the way you worship the Lord. I've also divided the conclusion into two important sections. First, there's a section for worshipers, which is for every one of us who are believers. Second, there's a section for worship leaders, which is specifically for those of us who are called to lead in worship as the church gathers faithfully for worship.

While the second section is focused on worship leaders, I hope that everyone will work through that section as well. It's helpful for worshipers and worship leaders to consider the application of God's Word to our gathered worship. I hope you'll use this concluding workbook section to assess and to plan your worship of the Lord on the inside and out.

Worshipers

(1) From chapter 1, what did God's Word reinforce about what you already knew about the essence of true worship?

(2) From chapter 1, what did God's Word remind you of when it comes to the essence of true worship?

(3) From chapter 1, what did God's Word reveal to you about the essence of true worship?

(4) From what God reinforced, reminded, and revealed to you in chapter 1, what does God want you to do in the way that you worship him?

(5) From chapter 2, what did God's Word reinforce about what you already knew about worship through offering and sacrifice?

(6) From chapter 2, what did God's Word remind you about concerning worship through offering and sacrifice?

(7) From chapter 2, what did God's Word reveal to you about worship through offering and sacrifice?

(8) From what God's Word reinforced, reminded, and revealed to you in chapter 2, what does God want you to do in the way you worship him through offering and sacrifice?

(9) From chapter 3, what did God's Word reinforce to you about worship in prayer?

(10) From chapter 3, what did God's Word remind you about when it comes to worship in prayer?

(11) From chapter 3, what did God's Word reveal to you about worship through prayer?

(12) From what God reinforced, reminded, and revealed to you in chapter 3, what does God want you to do in the way you worship him in prayer?

(13) From chapter 4, what did God's Word reinforce about worship in praise?

(14) From chapter 4, what did God's Word remind you of concerning worship in praise?

(15) From chapter 4, what did God's Word reveal to you about worship in praise?

(16) From what God's Word reinforced, reminded, and revealed to you in chapter 4, what does God want you to do in the way you worship him through praise?

(17) In chapter 5, what did God's Word reinforce to you about worship through the Word?

(18) In chapter 5, what did God's Word remind you about concerning worship through the Word?

(19) In chapter 5, what did God's Word reveal to you about worship through the Word?

(20) From what God's Word reinforced, reminded, and revealed to you in chapter 5, what does God want you to do in your worship through the Word?

(21) In chapter 6, what did God's Word reinforce to you about worship through the Lord's Supper?

(22) In chapter 6, what did God's Word remind you about concerning worship through the Lord's Supper?

(23) In chapter 6, what did God's Word reveal to you about worship through the Lord's Supper?

(24) From what God's Word reinforced, reminded, and revealed to you in chapter 6, what does God want you to do in your worship through the Lord's Supper?

Worship Leaders

(1) Considering chapter 1, assess the understanding and heart of worship in your church. What does your church understand well? What's not understood well about the essence of true worship?

(2) What are some ways that you can lead your church to grow in their understanding of the essence of biblical worship and to mature their hearts in true worship?

(3) Considering chapter 2, how well does your church understand and participate in biblical, New Testament worship in offering and sacrifice?

(4) What are some ways that you need to lead your church in worship through offering and sacrifice? What could this look like on a weekly basis as your church gathers for worship?

(5) Considering chapter 3, what does worship in prayer look like in your church when it gathers for worship? Is prayer routine and perfunctory, or is it responsive and participatory? Why?

(6) What are some ways that you need to lead your church to develop healthy, biblical worship through prayer in your gatherings?

(7) Considering chapter 4, what does worship through praise look like in your church? Is it driven more by tradition and preference or by biblical convictions and theology? Does it cater to preferences among groups in your church, or does it seek to reinforce unity in the family of God as the church comes together to worship?

(8) hat are some ways that you should lead your church to know and to obediently embrace worship through praise according to God's design for praise through song in his church? How could you teach biblical praise in your weekly worship services? How does it need to be practiced in your church?

(9) Considering chapter 5, what does worship through the Word look like in the worship services in your church? Is there an emphasis on the reading of Scripture? Is there sound teaching and preaching of the Scriptures? Is there accurate explaining and applying of the Scriptures? Is there an expectation for a response of belief and obedience to the Scriptures?

(10) What are some ways that worship through the Word needs to be taught to your congregation? How does participation in worship through the Word need to be reinforced on a weekly basis in your church?

(11) Considering chapter 6, does your church practice the Lord's Supper with regularity and purpose as communicated through God's Word? Is the Lord's Supper practiced under the understanding of its purpose as revealed in the Scriptures?

(12) What are some ways that you need to lead in observing the Lord's Supper in your church? What are some truths about the Lord's Supper that need to be taught and continually reinforced in your church?

Bibliography

Carson, D. A. *Worship by the Book*. Grand Rapids: Zondervan, 2002.

Chapell, Bryan. *Christ-Centered Worship: Letting the Gospel Shape Our Practice*. Grand Rapids: Baker Academic, 2016.

Davies, Horton. Christian Worship: Its Making and Meaning. Wallington: The Religious Education Press, 1957.

Getty, Keith, and Kristyn Getty. *Sing!: How Worship Transforms Your Life, Family, and Church*. Nashville: B & H Publishing Group, 2017.

Holy Bible: English Standard Version. Wheaton, IL: Crossway, 2001.

Johnson, Terry L. *Reformed Worship: Worship That Is According to Scripture*. Jackson, MS: Reformed Academic Press, 2010.

MacArthur, John. *Worship: The Ultimate Priority*. Chicago: Moody Publishers, 2012.

Merker, Matt. *Corporate Worship: How the Church Gathers As God's People*. Wheaton, IL: Crossway, 2021.

Parkison, Samuel G. *Revelation and Response: The Why and How of Leading Corporate Worship Through Song*. Spring Hill, TN: Rainer, 2018.

Piper, John. *Expository Exultation: Christian Preaching As Worship*. Wheaton, IL: Crossway, 2018.

Staff, Zondervan, Paul A. Basden, Stanley N. Gundry, Joe Horness, and Paul E. Engle. *Exploring the Worship Spectrum*. Grand Rapids: Zondervan, 2010.

Tozer, A. W. *Whatever Happened to Worship*. Chicago: Moody Publishers, 2012.

Webber, Robert. *Worship Old & New: A Biblical, Historical, and Practical Introduction*. Grand Rapids: Zondervan, 1982.

About the Author

Currently, Joel and his wife Tiffany have two adult children, one son-in-law, and one grandchild, who all live in Louisiana. Joel loves to preach and to teach God's Word, and he has the joy of serving the Lord as Senior Pastor at First Baptist Church in St. Francisville, Louisiana. Joel's teaching ministry extends from his church into the classroom both in Louisiana and internationally, where he teaches for New Orleans Baptist Theological Seminary (NOBTS). Joel holds a bachelor's degree from Louisiana Tech University, a master's degree from Louisiana State University, and a master's degree and doctoral degree from NOBTS.

www.ingramcontent.com/pod-product-compliance
Lightning Source LLC
Chambersburg PA
CBHW071458070526
44578CB00001B/382